Taken Up and Preached

Taken Up and Preached

A Collection of Biblical Sermons

BLAYNE A. BANTING

WIPF & STOCK · Eugene, Oregon

TAKEN UP AND PREACHED
A Collection of Biblical Sermons

Copyright © 2019 Blayne A. Banting. All rights reserved. Except for brief quotations in critical publications or reviews, no part of this book may be reproduced in any manner without prior written permission from the publisher. Write: Permissions, Wipf and Stock Publishers, 199 W. 8th Ave., Suite 3, Eugene, OR 97401.

Scripture quotations marked ESV are from The Holy Bible, English Standard Version* (ESV**), copyright © 2001 by Crossway Bibles, a publishing ministry of Good News Publishers. Used by permission. All rights reserved.

Scripture taken from THE MESSAGE. Copyright © 1993, 1994, 1995, 1996, 2000, 2001, 2002. Useds by permission of NavPress Publishing Group.

Wipf & Stock
An Imprint of Wipf and Stock Publishers
199 W. 8th Ave., Suite 3
Eugene, OR 97401

www.wipfandstock.com

PAPERBACK ISBN: 978-1-5326-9035-8
HARDCOVER ISBN: 978-1-5326-9036-5
EBOOK ISBN: 978-1-5326-9037-2

Manufactured in the U.S.A.   12/17/19

R. D. Scruggs Sr.
(1925–2019)

To the most memorable preacher from my childhood days,
whose voice seemed like the very voice of God to me
(just a little louder and a bit higher),
and who inspired me to find a voice of my own,
this book is dedicated with abiding affection and gratitude.

And to the loving and longsuffering members of Caronport
Community Church, Caronport, Saskatchewan,
who were the first recipients of these sermons,
thanks for your patience and encouragement.

Contents

Introduction	ix
1 ǀ Preaching Discursive Biblical Texts	1
"Catching Up to Our Calling"	3
"Bad News About the Good News"	8
"God's Gospel"	14
"Gospel Glue"	19
"Two Ways of Walking"	25
"This World Is Not Our Home"	31
"It's All in the Family"	36
"A Dream of Irresistible Influence"	42
"A Dream of Real Righteousness"	47
"A Dream of Intentional Obedience"	52
2 ǀ Preaching Poetic Biblical Texts	59
"Kiss the Risen Son!"	61
"A Wedding Fit for a King"	66
"When We Feel Depressed"	71
"When We Feel Surrounded"	76
"When We are Betrayed by a Friend"	82
"A Whole New Kind of Hero"	88
"What Happens When God Colors Outside the Lines?"	93
"Extreme Makeover: David's House Edition"	98
"Why Do You Reject Our Worship?"	103
"How Are We Robbing You?"	108

3	**Preaching Narrative Biblical Texts**	113
	"Why Did God Test Abraham?"	115
	"Why Did God Choose Jacob Over Esau?"	120
	"Take This Job and Love It"	125
	"The Jesus Cruise"	131
	"An Heir-Raising Adventure"	136
	"Lost and Found"	141
	"Party with a Purpose"	146
	"It Is Unfinished"	151
	"Emmaus Always Happens"	156
	"Prison Break"	161

Appendix   167

Bibliography   185

Introduction

THIS COLLECTION OF SERMONS represents a significant change in perspective for me. When I wrote *Take Up and Preach: A Primer for Interpreting Preaching Texts*, I went on record with my opinion that the written sermons found in homiletics books are often far less than exemplary and subtly encourage a mindset that looks at sermons as artifacts either to be analyzed or appreciated rather than events to be experienced. My nervousness in this regard remains, but that begs the question, "So then how do you propose to illustrate how your approach to preaching leads to an actual sermon and not just some abstract methodology?" Having students ask me, "So do you use your own method in your own preaching?" has made me reconsider. It only seems proper to demonstrate, however imperfectly, how I practice what I preach (or preach what I practice, as the case may be). This sermon collection is a response to this twinge of conscience and is designed to accompany *Take Up and Preach* as a companion volume for those who want to see how the Homiletical Bridge introduced there might lead to a full sermon.

While intended to accompany the method found in *Take Up and Preach*, these sermons might serve generally as samples of sermons that take the biblical text seriously. That is not to say they are necessarily praiseworthy examples or even represent what I consider to be my best work (as tenuous as judging one's own work can be), but they are real examples nonetheless. As I take pains to remind my students—there are no perfect sermons, just faithful (or unfaithful) ones. These sermons are taken from my own recent preaching ministry and therefore share in all the contextual idiosyncrasies of a given congregation and her preacher. You might notice how often song parodies occur in the following sermons—this is hardly to be taken as exemplary of good biblical preaching but is part of the implicit communication covenant between preacher and congregation.

INTRODUCTION

Your preaching ministry will be different (hopefully) and will exhibit the particularities of your own preaching context.

All written sermons are a bit like the proverbial frog in biology class. They help us learn about frogs, but they are dead. So, I have no designs for these sermons other than to serve the purpose of helping preachers get from the biblical text to the sermon. These sermons have been edited only to the degree that minor spelling and grammatical errors have been corrected and to bring these manuscripts closer to what I meant to say. In the end, these sermons are reproductions of my full sermon manuscripts and are not transcripts of the live sermons—so they are what I meant to say and not what I did say (preachers will be well-acquainted with the difference between the two). Most of the contextual idiosyncrasies remain and so there will be times when you might feel a bit "on the outside looking in" when there is insider information and running jokes that are part of the communication covenant between one congregation and her "off-the-wall" pastor. Since I have tried to illustrate these sermons more by personal and timely stories and events (rather than dust off the old books of illustrations which are overused and rather ineffective), much of their impact may be diminished by the time you read the sermon. That is inevitable—sorry. These sermons were originally accompanied by projected images since we live in a visual digital age. I have decided to omit the slides (except when it is necessary) and have inserted my editorial comments in square brackets where it seems helpful.

Barbara Brown-Taylor is right in calling her sermons "living room sermons," since every sermon should be directed toward those who sit around us in that space and time. Offering sermons given elsewhere is a bit like inviting complete strangers into your own living room and hoping they can make some sense of what is being said. It is in that spirit of hospitality that you are invited to have a seat and try to join in the conversation.

There are few tips you might need so you can take part in this interchange—vocabulary you will need to make sense of what is being said. There will be nothing new here, just a different dialect than you might be used to if you haven't read *Take Up and Preach*. Since a picture is worth a thousand words, we'll begin with a picture of the Homiletical Bridge. So, if you are familiar with this picture, feel free to skip this next part.

INTRODUCTION

Figure 1

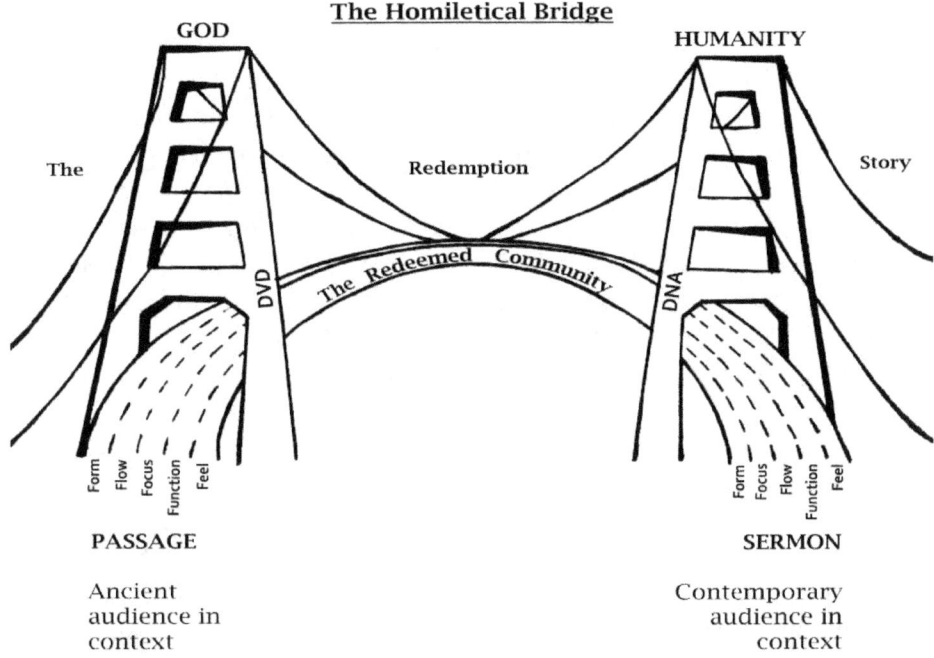

An Explanation of the Homiletical Bridge

THE CABLES OF THE BRIDGE

Cables that suspend this bridge could be compared to the grand story of redemption that anchor the bridge and extend well beyond both sides of the shore. The central affirmation of Scripture is the salvific purposes of the God who created, sustains, and will consummate all things. This is the grand story enacted throughout history and narrated throughout Scripture. There is a tendency for preachers to treat their texts in isolation from the rest of Scripture. Over time this communicates a rather disjointed view of the redemptive story line found in the Bible. To view every text and every sermon within the grand plot line of Scripture helps the preacher stay away from the errors of pitting the individual pericope against the whole of the canon and of a moralistic or anthropocentric emphasis.

Introduction

THE PYLONS OF THE BRIDGE

The cable superstructure rests securely upon two unchangeable pylons: God himself and the common traits and needs of humanity. That God be considered as one of these pylons can hardly be disputed. There is, by the way, no theological statement being made by having both God and humanity serve as pylons. I am in no way equating the two in terms of importance. The fact of the matter is, however, that we humans in our need are a common denominator between the text and the sermon. Notice the acronym DVD on the God pylon. The DVD is the *Divine Vision Disclosed* or, in other words, what do we see God doing, saying, or being in or around this text? What picture or vision of the triune God emerges from or around this text? This helps keep the emphasis where it belongs—with God, his words, and his desires.

The other pylon relates to our common human need—not our petty wants or desires but needs that are met ultimately in the gospel. Fred Craddock notes that "the distance between ourselves and the original readers of the text is in a measure bridged by our common humanity."[1] Note the acronym DNA on that pylon. It is the *Deep Need Addressed*. There are common matters of need that come from being sinful yet redeemed children of God, no matter what, where, and when we live.

THE BRIDGE DECK

Continuing the analogy, then, the bridge deck could be compared to the redeemed community, the connecting relationship of all who belong to God that runs through those chosen and redeemed by God throughout redemptive history. Allowing for differences in covenant and cultural context, we realize that we all are part of a larger family that is dependent upon the same Father for our spiritual well-being. This redeemed community keeps us from needlessly abstracting applications from the biblical context to our contemporary one. The same deep human need addressed by the text has been addressed by many others in this redeemed community over the years and in various contexts. To abstract an application from the biblical context directly to our own day overlooks how the text has affected countless other believers and congregations in between.

---

1. Craddock, *Preaching*, 134.

Introduction

The Homiletical Bridge requires that we, to some degree at least, walk over the bridge, appreciating how this same text has impacted others over the intervening centuries rather than simply jump from one side to the other. A broad diachronic (throughout history) and synchronic (other contemporary views) perspective helps us in understanding what the text might be saying and doing in our own congregation. So, we do not encounter a text to unearth that which is eternal or timeless but to discover the way(s) the message of the text is, for want of a better term, "bridgeable."

THE LANES ON THE BRIDGE

The five lanes on the Homiletical Bridge are arranged in a certain order on both the passage and sermon sides of the bridge. This order is not in terms of significance as all five are essential to the process. Nor should this order be followed rigidly as though it was the only way to encounter a text. Nor should the lanes be traversed in isolation from each other. They are all interrelated parts of the whole. The lanes on this bridge are marked by paint on pavement not by concrete meridians. A brief explanation of each lane follows.

The Form Lane

Preachers have long been aware of the importance of recognizing the text's form. I am using the term "form" in relation to its specific sub-genre (e.g., a doxology) rather the broader term "genre" (e.g., Epistle). My interest is not so much in the prehistory of the form (as in older types of form criticism) but in the rhetorical impact of these in the final form of the text. Each of these textual forms tends to have its own rhetorical strategy, its own way of getting its message across. Therefore, the text's form will have an effect on its meaning. So, the preacher will need to identify the form of the text as part of the exegetical-homiletical process. There is no precise methodology to follow here. For one thing, there is no standardized classification of forms used by all biblical scholars. The confusion in terminology can be quite perplexing at times. Also, the biblical writers are notorious for customizing these forms to fit their own purposes. Because of all these factors, our attempts to identify the form of the text will be somewhat tentative and imprecise. That is no excuse, however, for neglecting this necessary part of the task.

Introduction

The Flow Lane

I understand "flow" or movement in two senses: the macro and the micro. Every biblical passage is part of the flow or movement of a larger section to which it contributes in some way. This is the macro sense of the term or its larger literary context. Also, each passage has its own internal flow or movement (i.e., the micro sense) which Mike Graves defines as "the progression, structural pattern, or divisions of thought within a text."[2] Part of understanding the meaning of the text is following and analyzing this flow of thought. This flow will vary, of course, from form to form, and passage to passage. Then, in turn, the sermon will follow, at least in some connection, the flow of the passage. The sermon outline will need to demonstrate an essential connection to the flow of the text rather than be chosen from a predetermined list of outline options.

The Focus Lane

The choice of "focus" is purposeful (and not merely alliteratively convenient). Many homileticians prefer terms like: theme sentence, proposition, thesis statement, central idea, or big idea. The common denominator of these terms is that they all betray a certain emphasis on the cognitive aspect of "saying" with no mention of what the text might be "doing." Assuming the entire Bible communicates through clear, indicative statements (i.e., the proposition or big idea) may unnecessarily straitjacket those passages of Scripture which employ rhetorical strategies other than to inform. For example, to replace "taste and see that the LORD is good" (Ps 34:8) with "explain God's goodness" would not do justice to the text's rhetorical strategy. Such "cognitive cooking" of the text flattens the divine variety within biblical texts and makes all our sermons sound the same. There are some texts where this "big idea" approach is still helpful, but only where it intersects with the intended rhetorical strategy of the text. On other occasions, however, more holistic approaches are better.

Another unintentional implication of an overly didactic approach to the text is a dichotomy between explication (or explanation) and application. If the preacher is only encouraged to determine what the text is "about," the next step will require finding some way to apply it. That tends to result in an indicative-imperative split between exegesis and application.

---

2. Graves, *Sermon as Symphony*, 13.

Introduction

The result is that the preacher may struggle to relate the application to the exegetical explanation of the text. Sometimes the connection seems to be forced. As I have already intimated, there need not be that kind of dissonance between them. If the preacher remembers that the biblical writer's intention on every occasion may not be solely to instruct or argue, the explication-application dichotomy will be diminished.

The choice of "focus," then, allows for a little more latitude in understanding both what the text is saying and doing. It would be less restrictive to ask of the text, "What is the focus here?" rather than to ask, "What is the main idea here?"[3] "Focus" does, however, allow for a variety of rhetorical strategies.

The Function Lane

This is what the text intends to "do" to the reader. A text may inform the reader but also might warn, encourage, exhort, inspire, scold, or command. Most literary forms tend to have inherent rhetorical strategies (i.e., what we have termed a "function"), therefore there is a close relation between the text's form and function. For example, different forms of the gospel aphorism (saying) engage the reader differently: "A statement invites hearers to accept as true what Jesus asserts, a question seeks to engage hearers directly in pondering his saying, and an imperative challenges them to envision and act in line with the rhetorical force of his words."[4]

The purpose of a given text is more fully understood by what it says (i.e., its focus) *and* does (i.e., its function), so function has an important role to play in understanding this purpose. In the language of the Homiletical Bridge, the "focus" and the "function" (not to mention the "form," "flow," and "feel") give a fuller understanding of the author's purpose for the passage. The function and, in turn, the purpose (which would be the combination of the "focus" and the "function") of the sermon follows the lead of the text since "the preacher should attempt to say and do what a ...text *now* says and does for a new and unique set of people."[5]

---

3. Lowry, *How to Preach*, 173.
4. Bailey and Vander Broek, *Literary Forms*, 100.
5. Long, *Literary Forms*, 33.

Introduction

The Feel Lane

The feel (or mood/tone) of a text may be difficult to define but does contribute to the overall understanding of a text's meaning since it not only reflects the original author's purpose in writing the text but also "has to do with the emotional mood it creates."[6] This is not an attempt to determine the psychological motivation of the original author or the emotional response of the original audience to the text—these are almost impossible to determine. The feel is more a description of the emotive quality of the text which contributes to its intent. Again, it is important to note the close relationship between the lanes of form and function alongside feel. The form of the text will affect its function and the mood or feeling as well. Preachers may also need to be sensitive to the flow of a text as well. For example, in some psalms the feel or mood may change several times. The feel of the sermon, then, is to reflect the feel of the passage. Laments are to produce sermons that lament, doxologies call to praise, and miracle stories produce sermons that cause us to marvel at the God we serve.

Now we have a common vocabulary the conversation can begin. The sermons included in this collection have not been chosen for their brilliance but for their breadth of biblical textual forms. *Take Up and Preach* includes different methodologies for interpreting discursive, poetic, and narrative texts, therefore the following sermons are taken from each of these major types of biblical literature. The common practice in the church I served and from which all these sermons are taken is, at the appropriate time in the worship service, I would get up from among the congregation and make a few introductory remarks, ask the congregation to stand while I read the sermon text, lead in a prayer for illumination, ask them to be seated, and then I would dive into the sermon. That's the usual process and that is where each of the sermons in the book begins. You may also note that some sermons end by transitioning into the celebration of the Lord's Supper. So, welcome to my living room and feel free to join the conversation!

---

6. Long, *Literary Forms*, 134.

1

Preaching Discursive Biblical Texts

DISCURSIVE TEXTS ARE THOSE which communicate through some form of argumentation. That does not mean they are all polemic in nature, but they are all trying to be directly persuasive (i.e., to try to make a point[s]). Most readily we find these texts in the New Testament Epistles, but they are found scattered throughout the Bible (like the sermons in Acts and the Sermon on the Mount) and even some epistolary texts are not entirely discursive but poetic in form. Anywhere the biblical author wants to make a case for something, we have discursive literature. Any such discourse—whether found in Old or New Testament narrative, wisdom, prophecy or the book of Revelation—could be termed a discursive text. Usually these texts are direct in their argumentation and usually have a rather deductive flow to their development.

The preaching challenge in these texts can be to maintain enough tension to keep the congregation engaged until the end of the sermon. If they get there before the preacher does, that is a recipe for a chorus of yawns. Part of the preacher's task with texts like these is to be faithful to the text without being overly predictable. In my own context (a congregation in a village that worships in the facilities of a Christian college and seminary), part of my role was to challenge the perception that "we've heard this all before," so the congregation might be open to hearing the text with what Paul Ricoeur calls a "second naïveté."

"Catching Up to Our Calling"

Philippians 1:27–30, ESV
January 31, 2016

Series Title: "Joy in Our Journey"

PRAYER FOR ILLUMINATION

LORD, we are blessed beyond belief just because we can stand here and call you our LORD, our King, our Leader. We belong to you, we are yours and you are ours. That is the most important truth in the entire world. Forgive us when we don't live up to this awesome privilege. Show us more of what it means to seek your kingdom—here on earth as it is in heaven. And may the words of my mouth and the meditations of all our hearts be pleasing in your sight, O LORD, our Rock and our Redeemer. Amen.

SERMON

I've learned something from an old beer commercial. And now that I have your attention, let me tell you what I learned. I learned that I am Canadian. It's true. Whenever I hear the first few bars of O Canada, I want to stand at attention and take off my hat. I'm proud that we have the best Premier in the country. I'm proud that our prime minister has the coolest hair of any world leader (even if Donald Trump becomes the next president). (This statement proved to be accidentally prophetic.) I love seeing that big Canadian flag flying as I drive into Moose Jaw. I am Canadian.

But do you know when I am the most Canadian? It's when I'm not in Canada. That's when it hits me like a ton of bricks. I look around and realize, "I'm a foreigner!" It's different. They are speaking a different language.

Even when I go to the States and hear their version of what they think is English, I know I am away from home.

Last summer when I arrived in my hotel in Vietnam, I went into the bathroom and saw two bottles in the shower. One was shampoo and the other was conditioner, but I couldn't tell them apart—the labels were in Vietnamese. Since I don't think I need to bother with conditioner anymore, I took one of the bottles in one hand and my Vietnamese dictionary in the other and tried to figure it out. From what I could tell the bottle in my hand contained chocolate bananas. I don't think that was right, but just in case, I used the other bottle—chocolate bananas weren't going to touch this hair! Let's face it: I am Canadian—a big, white, monolingual Canadian!

I have a constant reminder of where I come from—it's called a passport. [Projected slide of my passport photo.] It is a reminder to every other country under heaven that all Canadians are ugly and apparently angry about something. But our passports do ground us somewhere.

Here's where we arrive at our text this morning. Paul has just been talking about his desire to come and see the Philippians once he gets out of prison. So now he says, "Only. . ." or so in the meantime, before I get there, "Let your manner of life be worthy of the gospel of Christ." Paul calls believers to this kind of behavior all the time, but he uses different words than he does here. Usually Paul calls the church to "walk" in a worthy manner—like in Ephesians 4:1. But here Paul doesn't use "walk," he uses a word that means to live as a citizen. So what Paul is calling for is for the Philippians and us to live as worthy citizens of the gospel of Christ.

Why the different word choice here? Remember who Paul is talking to—the Philippians. Remember Philippi is a Roman colony, very proud of its Roman status. They thought of themselves as "*picollo Roma*," a little Rome. In Philippi, living like a Roman is a very big deal.

Back when Paul first blew into town and was arrested for casting the demon out of the slave girl (Acts 16), the charge brought against him was that he was "advocating customs that are not lawful for us as Romans to accept or practice." So, when in Philippi, do as the Romans do.

So, what is Paul doing in this text? Paul is saying: live like worthy citizens of the gospel of Christ. He's telling them to get out their heavenly passports and take a good look. They do not belong there. They belong to the gospel. They are citizens of the gospel. Later in chapter 3, Paul says, "But our citizenship is in heaven, and from it we await a Savior [not a Caesar], the Lord Jesus Christ" (Phil 3:20).

"Catching Up to Our Calling"

This is our calling—to live as worthy citizens of the gospel. He's saying to us, "Look at your true passport—it doesn't say citizen of Canada—it says citizen of the gospel of Christ." Look at the picture, it's not our picture anymore, it's Jesus! That's awesome—I have hair!

We all have this same picture. We are all citizens of his gospel, his good news. This is Paul's call to us.

The question crossing your minds right now might be: "That's fine. We are called to be citizens of the gospel but how can we do that?"

I'm glad you asked, and so is Paul. He goes on to show us how. "So that whether I come and see you or am absent I may hear of you that you are standing firm in one spirit, with one mind striving side by side for the faith of the gospel, and not frightened in anything by your opponents."

The how of living as worthy citizens of the gospel is answered in what Paul wants to hear about the Philippians. It's by standing together for the gospel.

The reality of their situation and the reality of ours is that there will always be pressures put on us to cave in to the values of those around us. There were those in Philippi who were trying to force the church there to act like Romans. They had all the power of the surrounding culture and government behind them. It was making it hard for the Philippian Christians to maintain a distinct identity as citizens of the gospel. They were suffering for their faith. The pressure was on. They were viewed as outsiders, as non-conformists, radicals who didn't play along.

We don't have all the same pressures they had back then, but we do have our own. Even if we thought we once lived in a Christian country, no-one thinks that anymore. The facts say otherwise. Protestant Evangelicals have never comprised more than 8 percent of the Canadian population—right from the time of confederation. And even if we add the conservative Roman Catholic population of another 8 percent, that is still a small minority of the Canadian population. We don't call the shots anymore. Our commitments seem out of touch with the rest of our culture.

Now to believe that God's desire for marriage is between one man and one woman for life, or that all human life is a sacred gift from God, from the womb to the tomb, or that right and wrong are determined by God and not our own individual choices—that makes us old-fashioned and bigoted and self-righteous. We are called repressed, depressed, and obsessed. We may not be thrown in jail, but we are ridiculed, marginalized, and ostracized in many ways, sometimes subtly and sometimes blatantly.

It is not easy to be carrying another passport these days. And we don't know if it might just get harder. So how can we stand under that kind of pressure?

Paul is pretty clear—we need to stand together. This is not something we can or should do on our own. Paul talks about us "standing firm in one spirit." This probably means being united by the work of the same Holy Spirit—because this is how Paul normally uses this language and he will use it again in 2:1. To stand firm is to have your feet planted securely, to be steadfast.

Whenever I perform a marriage ceremony, I give instructions to the whole bridal party, but especially to the groomsmen. I tell them to hydrate and not to stand with their feet together. Otherwise they will topple over. One wedding, I had my nephew, who is 6' 7", keel over and take out half the bridal party, including the ring bearer.

We are to have one mind. The word translated "mind" is usually translated as "soul" or "life." It means to have the same attitude or focus. And then we are to be "striving side by side for the faith of the gospel."[1] Paul borrows a word from the arena of the gladiators—this is real striving, a life and death kind of striving. And we're doing all this side by side, not on our own but in a united and combined effort.

When we use this kind of fighting language, it's easy to get all pumped up and think we're out to take on the whole world—like we are mixed martial arts fighters in the cage match of the century. Easy on the testosterone! This striving is for the gospel. One scholar says, "Christians do not strive 'against' anybody (nor 'for' anybody either) but for the truth."[2]

There is no hint of triumphalism here—"Bring on the pagans and we'll whoop 'em good, real good." Our striving is not aggressive or offensive. We strive together in our suffering. Did you hear that? Our striving is by enduring suffering together. We win by pounding their fists with our faces until they give up. We don't fight like Ghengis Khan, we fight like Ghandi. We win just by hanging in there—together.

This may not be welcome news to us. We may want to ask Paul, "Why?" And he's ready for us. He's got three reasons why we are to strive together by our suffering together.

First, suffering is a sign that God is still in control. That seems absolutely backwards from the way we normally think. Paul says, "This is a

---

1. O'Brien, *Epistle to the Philippians*, 150.
2. Barth, *Epistle to the Philippians*, 47.

clear sign to them of their destruction but of your salvation and that from God." Normally, when we are suffering, we wonder where God is. We think suffering is evidence that God isn't in control. Our suffering is the sign that we haven't yet received our full reward and those who are persecuting us haven't received their full punishment. God has not lost control—we just can't tap out too soon.

Second, suffering is a gift to us. "For it has been granted to you that for the sake of Christ you should not only believe in him but also suffer for his sake." Paul uses "grace" language here. Suffering is a gracious gift to us from God. In the same way that we are graciously brought to believe in Christ, we are also graciously given the privilege to suffer for him. Paul says in chapter 3 that he wants to "know him and the power of his resurrection, and may share in his sufferings, becoming like him in his death, that by any means possible I may attain the resurrection from the dead" (Phil 3: 10–11). Whether we can understand it or not, suffering is a precious gift from God—when it comes from standing firm for the gospel.

And third, suffering binds us all together. Paul mentions to the Philippians that they are "engaged in the same conflict that you saw I had and now hear that I still have." As Christians we never suffer alone. The Philippians aren't suffering alone, because Paul is suffering with them. We never suffer alone because we have people right here who are suffering with us. We have fellow believers in Cuba, Syria, Iran, Iraq, and all over the world who suffer with us and we with them.

We can weather suffering and even welcome it when it comes from standing up for the gospel, because we do it together.

If the pressures around us break us apart and get each of us thinking about what is best for ourselves, then we fall. And the picture in our passports turns back into this ugly one that tells the world we would rather serve ourselves than the gospel of Christ. This does not come naturally. We need to be shown how to act together in unity—that's exactly what Paul will show us next week in chapter 2. But we know enough now to know we don't have to be ashamed of the ugly picture in our Canadian passports, but we can live as worthy citizens of the gospel of Christ by standing together as a loving yet somewhat messed up family. Because we may not have it all together, but together we have it all.

"Bad News About the Good News"

Galatians 1:1–10, ESV
May 7, 2017

*Series Title: "The Gospel in Galatians:
Nothing, More, Nothing Less, Nothing Else"*

PRAYER FOR ILLUMINATION

LORD we know all we have is from you. You have blessed us in so many ways. Yet there is something in us that is uncomfortable with grace. Somehow, we feel we should have to take matters into our own hands even though we know that always ends in disaster. Help us to learn how to embrace your grace, live in grace, serve in grace and love gracefully. And may the words of my mouth and the meditations of all our hearts be pleasing in your sight, O LORD, our Rock and our Redeemer. Amen.

SERMON

Have you ever changed your mind about something and then realized you probably should have stuck with your first impression? It's like thinking that big tattoo of your current girlfriend's name is a good idea after all. Or maybe I should buy that new VCR. Or maybe it's a good career move to take the job as the guy who catches the javelins during the Olympics.

Earlier this week, I was playing volleyball over lunch hour. I served the ball, and when our friend Jeanette Olney tried to return the serve, it fractured a bone in her thumb. What was my first reaction? I was mortified. It's obviously a bad situation—I shouldn't be doing those kinds of things. They have nasty consequences.

"Bad News About the Good News"

But after a day or so, I started to change my mind. Man, that must have been a killer serve. What power! I am awesome!

See what happened? I went from "I can't do this sort of thing" to "Yes, I can, and I'm amazing." I should have stuck with my first impression.

That's a bit like what happens to the Galatian Christians all those centuries ago. The apostle Paul came to their province (which is in modern day Turkey) on his first missionary journey and preached the gospel to them and planted several churches in the area. And after he leaves, there are some Jewish Christians who arrive on the scene and start undoing what Paul has done.

Most of the new Christians in these Galatian churches are gentiles; they were not Jews before they responded to the gospel. So, these Jewish Christians are telling them that to be a true follower of Jesus they need to follow Jesus, and they need to follow him fully by living like Jewish people. That would mean being circumcised and obeying the Jewish food laws and all that was part of being Jewish.

These Galatian Christians started well but now they are having second thoughts about what it means to embrace the gospel. Paul hears about all this and fires off this letter to set the record straight. And as you might have noticed, he's got his toga in a twist about what he's heard.

The big issue in this letter is the gospel. If we don't get this right, then nothing is right. If we don't get the gospel right, we will lose the unity of the church. We won't know how to live as followers of Jesus in the power of the Holy Spirit. We won't understand what it means to live in freedom and we won't appreciate the ministry of the apostle Paul either. It all rests on the gospel—this good news of Jesus Christ.

This is what Paul is saying to us as well: it's all about the gospel—nothing more, nothing less, and nothing else.

We can get what Paul is talking about right from the very beginning of this letter. It's like one of those "I've got good news and I've got bad news situations." Like when the doctor comes in after surgery and says, "I've got good news and bad news, which would you like first?" You say, "Start with the bad," so he says, "The bad news is that we amputated the wrong leg. But the good news is the other leg is perfectly healthy!"

So, first the good news.

> ¹ Paul, an apostle—not from men nor through man, but through Jesus Christ and God the Father, who raised him from the dead—
> ² and all the brothers who are with me,

To the churches of Galatia:

> ³ Grace to you and peace from God our Father and the Lord Jesus Christ, ⁴ who gave himself for our sins to deliver us from the present evil age, according to the will of our God and Father, ⁵ to whom be the glory forever and ever. Amen. (Gal 3:1–5)

You can tell a lot about a letter by how it starts. If you get a letter and it begins with "To my darling love muffin," you are expecting this letter is from your true love, right? But if that letter is from your banker, it's time to get a new banker. If you get a letter that starts with "Dear occupant," you are expecting something impersonal—maybe from your banker. But if it's from your true love, then it's probably time to get a new true love. See what I mean?

This is how Paul does it. His greetings are meaningful. They are like teasers or movie trailers, giving a taste of what is to come.

So, he begins by introducing himself: "Paul, an apostle—not from men, nor through men, but through Jesus Christ and God the Father, who raised him from the dead—and all the brothers who are with me."

Why start the letter this way? Did you notice anything? Does he sound a little defensive to you? Apparently, he thinks the best defense is a good offense and he's going to head all this off at the pass. Paul wants us to know who he is—one commentator says he wants to show he's an apostle and not an imposter. The gospel he's preached is under fire and so are his credentials as an apostle. He's not one of the original Twelve, so why should these Christians listen to him anyway? Why should we listen to him? It's because it is God who has commissioned him to be an apostle—not any kind of human authority or church council—it is God who has made Paul an apostle. Paul's ministry has come from God.

Now we have this straight, Paul addresses the churches: "To the churches of Galatia: Grace and peace from God our Father and the Lord Jesus Christ, who gave himself for our sins to deliver us from the present evil age, according to the will of our God and Father, to whom be glory forever and ever. Amen" (Gal 1:6–10). Notice what Paul does here: he includes the basic content of the gospel right in his greeting. He wishes them grace and peace like he always does, but then he goes on as if to say, "And here is how you have received this grace and peace." This is a bumper sticker version of the gospel.

Notice that it begins and ends with God our Father. The gospel, this good news, was God's idea in the first place—it was according to his will.

"Bad News About the Good News"

And it ends with God because the gospel brings glory to God forever and ever. This gospel is about Jesus "who gave himself for our sins." And it's for us "to deliver us from the present evil age."

So, this is the true gospel in a nutshell: It is from God's will and to God's glory; it is about Jesus and his death for our sins; and it's for us to deliver us from the present evil age. Now we all know what Paul means when he talks about the gospel.

God, through the death of Christ for us, has graciously rescued us from this old dead end way of life dedicated to worship of self. And he has made us his children, so we are free to love and serve him and each other.

And this is not just something God has done in the narrow confines of our own hearts. This is something God has done on a cosmic scale. The good news of the death and resurrection has rocked the entire universe. In the gospel, God is announcing something new. That is why it's called good news. The good part of the good news is all wrapped up in God.

And now for the bad news.

> ⁶ I am astonished that you are so quickly deserting him who called you in the grace of Christ and are turning to a different gospel— ⁷ not that there is another one, but there are some who trouble you and want to distort the gospel of Christ. ⁸ But even if we or an angel from heaven should preach to you a gospel contrary to the one we preached to you, let him be accursed. ⁹ As we have said before, so now I say again: If anyone is preaching to you a gospel contrary to the one you received, let him be accursed.
>
> ¹⁰ For am I now seeking the approval of man, or of God? Or am I trying to please man? If I were still trying to please man, I would not be a servant of Christ (vv. 6–10).

Verses 6 and 7: "I am astonished that you are so quickly deserting him who called you in the grace of Christ and are turning to a different gospel—not that there is another one, but there are some who trouble you and want to distort the gospel of Christ."

Usually after his greeting, Paul thanks God for the recipients of the letter or prays for them—but not this time. No time to waste on niceties.

Paul wastes no time in expressing his feelings. I get this sense that Paul probably wouldn't make a great counsellor—no reflective listening, no unconditional personal regard—he just lets them have it. "I'm astonished, shocked, flabbergasted, scandalized, dumbfounded, completely amazed, and blown away in a bad way that you could have changed your minds so quickly."

Paul isn't angry that they have forgotten him or that they are disrespecting him, even though he was the one who preached the gospel to them in the first place. It isn't him they are deserting—it's God: "you are so quickly deserting *him* who called you in the grace of Christ."

When we mess with the gospel, we are messing with God and his grace. That's why Paul says this twice: "If anyone tries to gospelize or evangelize anyone with a different gospel, they are under God's curse." That includes, angels, Paul himself, smooth-talking, miracle-working televangelists, megachurch pastors, our favorite Bible teachers, or theologians.

If we distort the grace of the gospel, we are denying God's ability to save us. We are putting ourselves in God's place. That is why that brings God's curse down on us.

So how serious is this curse? Maybe you remember from the Old Testament when Israel was entering the promised land. The Canaanites were so wicked that God said their entire cities needed to be devoted to destruction—completely obliterated. This is the same idea. Those who distort the gospel are dedicated to destruction.

So, whenever we stop thinking "God's got this" and start thinking, "I've got this" we are distorting the gospel of God's grace.

And when we distort the gospel, we desert God. You'll notice all the good parts of the good news relate to God: it's from God; it's about God. All the bad parts of the gospel have to do with us—we are the reason for this needed rescue, and we are the ones prone to distort the news when God comes to our rescue.

That's why Paul says he's not trying to please other people by preaching what they might want to hear. He views himself as a servant (literally a slave) of Christ.

So how might all this relate to us today? Is there a chance we are distorting the gospel? What does it mean for us to distort the gospel?

Whenever we deny the grace of God in our lives and try to rely on our own efforts, we distort the gospel. Whenever we can't understand why Jesus would love us so much he would die for our sins—when we are mystified and skeptical of grace, we subtly distort the gospel.

There is a scene in *Beauty and the Beast* when Belle has tracked down her father—crazy old Maurice—to the dungeon in the Beast's castle. Maurice is being held for trespassing and so Belle says, "Take me instead!"

"Bad News About the Good News"

The Beast is baffled by this and says, "You would take his place?"

"If I did, would you let him go?" Belle bargains.

"Yes, but you must promise to stay here forever," answers Beast.

"You have my word," Belle vows.

"Done!"

The Beast has no idea what has just happened—but we do. Grace has just happened.

It takes some of us longer than others to awaken to grace, but when we do, we will be amazed that God has always been there, and he never tires in showering us with undeserved grace.

It's a tale as old as time, a song as old as rhyme: when our bad news is turned into good news by the One who has given himself for our rescue. Not only should this grab our attention—it should inspire our faithful praise.

"God's Gospel"

Galatians 1:11–24, ESV
May 14, 2017

*Series Title: "The Gospel in Galatians:
Nothing More, Nothing Less, Nothing Else"*

PRAYER FOR ILLUMINATION

Almighty Father, you are maker of heaven and Earth. You are the giver of all good gifts. Everything comes from you and comes back to you. We are blessed to be your children, to have received from you all that we are and all we have. Remind us once more of how we might respond to your grace. And may the words of my mouth and the meditations of all our hearts be pleasing in your sight, O LORD, our Rock and our Redeemer. Amen.

SERMON

Two guys come to church to worship. One stands right up at the front for everyone to see. He lifts his hands to heaven and says, "Here I am Lord just like I've been here every Sunday for thirty years and never missed once. I've been a leader in this church for decades and even took a shot at teaching the junior high boys Sunday school class. I give a tithe and support ten missionaries besides. I live by the book, sing out of a book and pray out of a book. I am a paragon of virtue. I'm here, now church can start!"

The other guy slumps in the back row and can just mumble under his breath, "Lord, I'm a mess—have mercy on me!"

One of these guys left changed. Guess which one.

"God's Gospel"

If you're a student of the Bible, you probably recognized this story as a contemporary version of Jesus' parable of the publican and the Pharisee, or as I like to call it, the parable of the publican and the Republican. (That's just to make sure all you Americans are still awake.)

This story is related to the story of Galatians, but it's not identical. This parable addresses how we *get into* God's family. Paul is talking to the Galatians about how we *get along in* God's family. The answer to both issues is the same, by the way: it's the gospel of grace.

Maybe you remember that Paul had planted these churches in the province of Galatia and, soon after he left, some Jewish Christians came along telling the churches that Paul had been soft-selling the gospel. To be part of God's family, they say, you not only have to trust in Jesus, but you have to live like a Jewish person, complete with circumcision and all the dietary laws, etc. They are preaching this message like it was Gospel 2.0, and Paul responds by saying it's not good news at all. All this stuff added onto faith in Christ is good enough to keep you out of jail, but not good enough to keep you out of hell (in the words of David Platt).[3]

So how is Paul going to make his case to these new Christians? How is he going to show there is only one true gospel?

His answer comes in verses 11 and 12: "For I would have you know, [we should know by this that Paul is about to tell us something very important] brothers, that the gospel that was preached by me (literally 'the gospel that was 'gospelled' by me') is not man's gospel. For I did not receive it from any man, not was I taught it, but I received it through a revelation of Jesus Christ (or by Jesus being reveled to me)."

This is Paul's argument: the gospel comes from God. The gospel he preached to them wasn't something secondhand or second rate, it came directly from God to him. It was purely a God thing.

It's one thing to say this is purely a God thing or God told me to do this or that. It's another to prove it. How do we know God told you this? What if you just had some bad tuna?

It's not that this hasn't happened before to God's people. Picture Noah looking out the window of the ark at all his neighbors doing the dogpaddle and saying, "Sorry guys, it's a God thing," or Joshua trying to explain the walls of Jericho falling in, "Whoa, I know, right? It must be a God thing." Or Moses coming down the mountain with the Ten Commandments, "Look

---

3. Platt and Merida, *Exalting Jesus in Galatians*, 23.

what I got guys! It must be a God thing." Or Mary talking to Joseph: "Guess what? I'm pregnant—it's a God thing."

So, this is how Paul does it: he is going to show that the gospel comes from God by telling his own story. He doesn't try to use some sophisticated theological argument, he just tells his own story. But this is not just another personal testimony. Paul tells his own story with a purpose in mind. He tells it to show he did not receive the gospel from anyone else, but it came to him right from God. The gospel is a God thing.

So, this is what Paul is saying: the gospel comes from God, but it spreads through us.

For the rest of this text, Paul tells us his personal testimony—what he was like before he met Jesus, how he met Jesus, and what happened since he met Jesus.

We get this picture of Paul before coming to Jesus in verses 13 and 14: "For you have heard of my former life in Judaism, how I persecuted the church of God violently and tried to destroy it. And I was advancing in Judaism beyond many of my own age among my people, so extremely zealous was I for the traditions of my fathers."

So, this is a picture of Paul before he encountered Jesus. Suffice it to say, when he graduated from rabbinical school in Jerusalem, he was not voted most likely to become a church planter. He was hardly a planter, he was persecutor and a frenzied, driven one at that. He was a keener, an up-and-comer in the rabbinical ranks, a confirmed religious terrorist. His name struck fear into the hearts of every believer in Jerusalem.

In his own words, Paul says he "persecuted the church of God *violently* and tried to destroy it." The word "violently" is where we get our "hyperbole," or intentional exaggeration. It means Paul persecuted the church excessively, or beyond measure. It was overkill, over-the-top, and out-of-control.

This is not the kind of person you would normally pick to be a preacher of the gospel. But God has this weird way about him.

I'm not saying we all need to be just like Paul because we aren't, and that's not Paul's point anyway. But we share something in common with Paul—we have a "before coming to Jesus" part of our lives. Maybe some of us are still there. The fact of the matter is we all start from the same place—without Jesus and without hope. We don't need a story that would make a policeman blush. I don't have a story like that. I came to Jesus when I was nine. I was a pretty nice kid. I wasn't even all that good at sinning yet, but I still needed Jesus.

"God's Gospel"

Then we come to the "coming to Jesus" part in verses 15 and 16a: "But when he who had set me apart before I was born, and who called me by his grace, was pleased to reveal his Son to me, in order that I might preach him among the Gentiles."

Three little English words—"but when he"—are the words that turn Paul's story around. And they turn our story around as well.

The emphasis is on God—it's Paul's conversion, but the emphasis is on God. That shouldn't surprise us really. After all, this letter of Galatians is about grace, and grace comes from God.

Notice what Paul says here about God's work in his own story of coming to faith. He's not trying to give us a sacred order of how everyone comes to faith necessarily. Remember, he's telling his story to show the gospel has come directly from God, not himself.

So, God chose him or set him apart from before he was born and called him by his grace. This makes it sound like Paul didn't have much of a choice in the matter, did he? God had already stacked the deck in favor of Paul's coming to Christ. And, yes, God does choose and call people to himself but that's not Paul's point here either. You might hear whispers of how God called Isaiah and Jeremiah as prophets who were to receive direct revelation from God. Paul is not trying to say, "See, I came to faith just like everyone else does"—he's trying to say, "I was called to receive this direct news from God just like the prophets were."

Notice he was called by God's grace and not steamrolled by God's power. Grace doesn't save us against our will but according to God's will. Grace is not God mugging us, grace is God hugging us.

There's more. God was pleased to reveal Jesus to Paul—also making the point that Paul got the gospel directly from God.

God has a purpose in mind with all this: "in order that I might preach him (Jesus) to the Gentiles." Paul came to Jesus so that he could preach the good news to the gentiles—those who he had preached to in the Galatian churches. Not only had God given him what to say, God had given him a reason to say it—God wanted him to.

Paul tells us how he came to faith so that we would believe what he says to us. That's his point.

We know we're not Paul. We may not have come to Jesus the same way Paul did—maybe most of us haven't. But we do have one thing in common with Paul. We, too, were all saved for a purpose. Maybe it isn't to preach to the gentiles, maybe it is. But we are saved for something greater than ourselves. Paul was fulfilling that in his life. We are called to fulfill our purpose in our own lives.

Paul spends the rest of his time talking about what happened after coming to Jesus.

Paul fills in the blanks of his actions after coming to Jesus, but he's not trying to give us the whole story. He's just trying to show he didn't get the gospel secondhand from anyone—it came from God.

Right after coming to Jesus Paul doesn't try to figure out what had just happened to him. Rather than enroll in the Jerusalem Theological Seminary, he spends three years in seclusion in Arabia and Damascus. Only then does he go up to Jerusalem, and even then, he only spent a few days with a couple of guys—Peter and James, the brother of Jesus. Then he goes back to his home territory of Cilicia so he's been invisible to the believers around Jerusalem.

Paul says this is to show he was not commissioned by the church in Jerusalem and, as a matter of fact, they wouldn't even recognize him in person. All they knew was that the persecutor had turned into a preacher, the terrorist had become an evangelist, and all they could do was glorify God.

Not only was he given the gospel straight from God, but his own life was the greatest proof that this gospel could only be from God.

The greatest proof of the gospel is a transformed life. Paul's life didn't need tweaking—it needed transforming. That's what the gospel does.

Many of you may have heard of Lee Strobel. He was an avowed atheist and award-winning editor at the *Chicago Tribune*, but his life was a mess. He was profane and angry at life. He had a little daughter named Allison. Strobel would come home night after night in a rage—one night he kicked his foot right through the wall. All Allison could do was hide in her room.

When Allison was five, Strobel came to Jesus. Five months later, Allison went to her mother and said, "Mommy, I want God to do for me what he's done for Daddy."

The greatest proof of God's gospel is what it can do in and through us.

"Gospel Glue"

Galatians 2:1–10, ESV

May 21, 2017

*Series Title: "The Gospel in Galatians:
Nothing More, Nothing Less, Nothing Else"*

PRAYER FOR ILLUMINATION

O LORD you are one God—Father, Son, and Holy Spirit. That mystifies us, but it also inspires us. It leaves us speechless and makes us want to shout your praises. It makes us long to be unified and thankful for our amazing diversity. Help us to live in the image of who you are and what you are calling us to be. And may the words of my mouth and the meditations of all our hearts be pleasing in your sight, O LORD, our Rock and our Redeemer. Amen.

SERMON

When you get up in the morning and stumble into the bathroom and squint at the mirror through your sleepy eyes—what do you see? You see your face. We all have one—some of us may even have two of them!
Our faces are important to us—whether we like it or not. Our faces are the center of four of our five senses. Our face is the window into our soul. We have to face the past, face the future; we may lose face or save face; we may have to face failure, or face the music. Some of us spend way too much time putting on our face and some of us don't spend enough time. Most of us have a love-hate relationship with our faces.

Let's face it—we are a bit preoccupied with our faces. This may come as a surprise to us, but people back in Paul's time were even more so. It resulted from being in a different culture. They were part of a shame-based culture where the greatest good was to save face or to receive honor in the face of everyone else. The greatest fear was they might lose face or be shamed in the face of others. Because of this, every social situation became a face off—a contest to see who would save face and who would lose it. What Paul says in this text doesn't make much sense unless we get this.

This is the second of three stories Paul tells us to show us there is only one gospel. We looked at the first story last week, and Pastor Josh will look at the third one next week. Last week we looked at Paul's conversion and these next two stories are pivotal ones in Paul's own story that show us something about the true gospel. Actually, these stories are two important showdowns ("verbal cage matches" to you violent ones in the crowd) that are make-or-break episodes in the history of the early church. If they go south, then the gospel goes with it.

Today we look at a three-sided showdown. On one side are Paul, Barnabas, and Titus; on another are the pillars of the Jerusalem church: Peter, James, and John (a different James from the Gospels because that one had already been martyred); and on the third side are some of these teachers who are saying everyone must become Jewish (including being circumcised and obeying the Jewish laws) if they want to become full believers in Jesus.

There's a lot going on here, and since we weren't there in person, we're probably not going to catch all that happens. Basically, Paul makes his case, is opposed by these false teachers, and then the conflict is resolved. We've already read the text, so we know what happens in the end. Two of the sides save their faces: Paul and his buddies and the leaders of the Jerusalem church. One side ends up losing face—the false teachers. Spoiler alert!

Normally we should understand a story the way stories are to be understood—by looking at the characters and how the plot unfolds. But Paul is telling this story in a letter—to make a point—so that's what we're going to try to do.

What *is* the point? Why does Paul tell us this story? Here's a hint—it's about God. The real hero in this cage match is outside the cage. So, let's see what Paul tells us about God and then the rest may fall into place for us.

"Gospel Glue"

Remember, Paul has already said the gospel comes from God and God has given it directly to Paul—that's territory we've already covered in the last two weeks.

The first thing we see is that God doesn't play favorites.

> Then after fourteen years I went up again to Jerusalem with Barnabas, taking Titus along with me. ² I went up because of a revelation and set before them (though privately before those who seemed influential) the gospel that I proclaim among the Gentiles, in order to make sure I was not running or had not run in vain. ³ But even Titus, who was with me, was not forced to be circumcised, though he was a Greek. ⁴ Yet because of false brothers secretly brought in—who slipped in to spy out our freedom that we have in Christ Jesus, so that they might bring us into slavery— ⁵ to them we did not yield in submission even for a moment, so that the truth of the gospel might be preserved for you. ⁶ And from those who seemed to be influential (what they were makes no difference to me; God shows no partiality)—those, I say, who seemed influential added nothing to me (vv. 1–6).

Here's the thing: In Paul's day, social status is everything. You didn't rock the boat. If you had a lower status, you didn't try to mess with anyone above you on the food chain because that would shame them and make them lose face. Paul is marching right into the mother church in Jerusalem to talk to those who are the respected leaders: Peter, James and John.

He makes it perfectly clear that he is not going to Jerusalem because the leaders there had called him to explain what he had been doing. He went there because God had told him to go by revealing it to him.

And Paul is bringing Titus with him, a non-Jewish believer in Jesus who has not been circumcised. This is a real gutsy move. Everyone in the Jerusalem church is Jewish and bringing Titus right into the middle of them is making a huge statement. This would be seen as socially scandalous. Who does Paul think he is?

Notice how Paul refers to Peter, James, and John: three times he refers to them as those "who seemed influential," and once as those "who seemed to be pillars." Doesn't that sound a least a little cheeky? He sounds like he's talking behind his hand a lot in this text. Who is he to say that about these respected leaders in the church? This is way out of line. He sounds a little like a college freshman bursting into the dean's office with a list of demands, that if not fulfilled, he's going back to his mom and dad.

Paul tips his hand in verse 6 in what is another "behind the hand" comment: "what they were makes no difference to me; God shows no partiality." Bam, there it is. Paul is not acting this way because he has bad manners or no social graces. He does this because of who God is. God plays no favorites. Literally Paul uses a Hebrew figure of speech here: "God does not lift the face." Back in OT times, when God wanted to favor or honor someone he would lift their face. To not lift the face means God does not show favoritism. God doesn't do face lifts.

This is the whole ball game. There will be one gospel only if God does not play favorites. There will be one church only if God does not play favorites. Because God looks at all of us the same way and wants the same thing for all of us, he gives us his one gospel and brings us into his one church.

Paul's real issue is not with Peter, James, and John—he is coming there to make sure he is on the same page as they are—that all are preaching the same gospel. And they are. Hallelujah! They added absolutely nothing to Paul's message. As a matter of fact, Peter, James, and John went further to give Barnabas and Paul the right hand of fellowship. This is more than just a polite gesture—it is a ritual of partnership. It cements the fact they are all on the same team—with the same gospel and in the same church.

Paul is not opposed to Peter, James, and John—they are on the same team, they are bros. But Paul is against somebody and he describes them in verses 4 and 5: "Yet because of false brothers secretly brought in—who slipped in to spy out our freedom that we have in Christ Jesus so that they might bring us into slavery—to them we did not yield in submission even for a moment, so that the truth of the gospel might be preserved for you."

These were the guys who wanted to add to the gospel—not Peter, James, and John. They wanted to add the Jewish laws and customs of circumcision to the gospel. To them the gospel was a message about Jesus and Moses. Paul doesn't call that a full gospel, he calls that slavery, a distortion of the gospel.

The moment anyone adds anything to the gospel of Jesus they take us back to slavery. We need to remember that theme of slavery because it will show up again several times in the rest of the book of Galatians. The moment we add anything to the gospel—whether that be our view of the end times, the role of women, how the church is to be organized, a certain music style, or the gifts of the Holy Spirit—we have done the very same thing. The truth of the gospel is Jesus, not Jesus and Moses, or Jesus

"Gospel Glue"

and Pope Francis, or John Calvin, or John Wesley, or John Piper, or Martin Luther, or A.B. Simpson. The true gospel is Jesus—just Jesus.

This is God's gospel—the glue that keeps us together. Anyone who messes with that glue with eventually come unglued.

But there is something else we learn about God in this text as well. We see that God gives us different ministries.

> ⁷ On the contrary, when they saw that I had been entrusted with the gospel to the uncircumcised, just as Peter had been entrusted with the gospel to the circumcised ⁸ (for he who worked through Peter for his apostolic ministry to the circumcised worked also through me for mine to the Gentiles), ⁹ and when James and Cephas and John, who seemed to be pillars, perceived the grace that was given to me, they gave the right hand of fellowship to Barnabas and me, that we should go to the Gentiles and they to the circumcised. ¹⁰ Only, they asked us to remember the poor, the very thing I was eager to do (vv. 7–10).

In the end, it looks like Paul is free to spread the gospel to the non-Jewish peoples just like he has done to the Galatians, and Peter and the others could go on preaching the gospel to the Jewish people. After all this talk about one God who has one gospel and one church, this might seem a bit like a disappointing outcome. Why didn't they all preach the gospel to both the Jewish and non-Jewish people and join hands and sing forty-two verses of "Kum Ba Yah"?

The reason they didn't do this is because of God. The same God who doesn't play favorites gives different people different ministries. That's the way God does it. God doesn't make us like we are cookies—all cut out with the same shape. He makes us like snowflakes—everyone's unique.

Let me read verses 7-9 emphasizing the God parts of these verses:

> On the contrary, when they saw that *I had been entrusted* with the gospel to the uncircumcised, just as Peter *had been entrusted* (not included but assumed in the original) to the circumcised (for *he who worked* through Peter for his apostolic ministry to the circumcised *worked* also through me for mine to the Gentiles) and when James and Cephas and John, who seemed to be pillars, perceived the grace that was given to me, they gave the right hand of fellowship to Barnabas and me, that we should go to the Gentiles and they to the circumcised.

It's not two different gospels, it's just one gospel in two different ministries. Here's the good news. We are not supposed to be the same. I'm not supposed to be like you and you're not supposed to be like me. Isn't that awesome? You bet your life it is. We are all free to serve in way he's gifted us to. We don't measure ourselves according to who has the most power or authority. It's not about face, it's about grace.

So, here's what we learned today: God doesn't play favorites and he gives us different ministries. If we put these together, we get what Paul is saying to us: God's one gospel makes one free people. We are free from a life of rule-keeping, and we are free to serve as God has called us to. But this grace to serve as we've been gifted is no excuse to fracture his one gospel and his one church. Our different gifts are part of that same gospel glue that holds us together as sisters and brothers in Christ.

One of my favorite stories is told by Haddon Robinson about a tour given in an asylum for the criminally insane. This guy is being shown around by an armed guard and when they were through, he asks the guard, "I saw hundreds of very dangerous people but only a few armed guards. Aren't you afraid they will get together and overpower you?" The guard looks at him and says, "Lunatics never unite." Politically correct? Probably not. But correct? Without a doubt.

"Two Ways of Walking"

Galatians 5:13—6:10, ESV
July 9, 2017

*Series Title: "The Gospel in Galatians:
Nothing More, Nothing Less, Nothing Else"*

PRAYER FOR ILLUMINATION

LORD, we thank you for your forgiving grace in our lives. We also thank you for the grace that empowers us to do what you want us to. Sometimes we forget that being able to follow you is as much grace and being forgiven by you. Help us to learn to walk in this grace to your glory. And may the words of my mouth and the meditations of all our hearts be pleasing in your sight, O LORD, our Rock and our Redeemer. Amen.

SERMON

We were in Calgary this week for a few days. I was there with the three women in our family. I voted we go to Banff. We went to IKEA. If you have never been to an IKEA store before, there is nothing that warns you what you are about to step into. From the outside, it looks just like any other big box store. It looks friendly enough—blue and yellow—the calming colors of Sweden. (And everyone knows the Swedish wouldn't hurt anyone—ask Don Cherry.) Appearances can be deceiving. This welcoming exterior is hiding an honest-to-goodness testosterone-sucking mantrap. Miles of meandering paths through piles of household goods. Every item in the store has its own name and each one is calling *your* name. It's endless and cavernous. And addictive. By the time we made it out of there, our SUV was stacked to the roof and we had stuff strapped to the roof rack. We drove uphill all the way home to Caronport.

I learned one expensive lesson from my trip to IKEA. There are two ways to walk through an IKEA store. One is pushing a big shopping cart, filling it as you go. The other way is to walk through with your arms crossed, refusing to buy a thing. People notice if that's what you do. I call it the walk of shame.

Paul talks about two ways of walking too—right here as he gets very near to the end of his letter to the churches in the province of Galatia or what we know as modern Turkey.

Paul has been addressing key themes throughout this letter: the gospel, grace, freedom, and how they all relate to the unity of the church. Now he gets to the part when he starts to wrap them all up with some practical guidance. He's spent time with the "what"—safeguarding the gospel from those who would add obedience to the Jewish law to faith in Jesus. He also has dealt with the "so what" because he has shown us the consequences of this kind of false teaching. Now he heads to the "now what" part of the letter where he helps us apply what he has been talking about.

All the way through the letter, Paul has been showing the contrast between the true gospel of Jesus Christ and the false "gospel" of his opponents. So, it's not a big stretch to see the contrast between two ways of walking that Paul makes here.

When Paul talks about walking, he means how we live our lives. He's reaching back into his past training as a rabbi where they talk about life as a journey and how we live life by walking it in the right way.

Paul takes us from true freedom, what Pastor Andrew preached about last week, to how that freedom is to be applied within the life of our church. Here's how Paul connects freedom with how we are supposed to live:

Verses 13–15: "For you were called to freedom, brothers. Only do not use your freedom as an opportunity for the flesh; but through love serve one another. For the whole law is fulfilled in one word: "You shall love your neighbor as yourself." But if you bite and devour one another, watch out that you are not consumed by one another."

Here's Paul's command to us in a nutshell: Don't walk alone.

Paul is critiquing a false view of freedom. People back then (and certainly today) thought freedom was the right to do whatever they wanted to with no restrictions. It's a very self-focused idea. Paul turns this idea on its head.

"Two Ways of Walking"

For starters, he's not even talking to individuals, he's talking to the whole church. Freedom is not an individual right. Freedom is a gift to be enjoyed in the company of others. And even more radical than that, "through love serve one another"—freedom is shown by how we serve others. The verb for "serve" here means to serve as a slave. This should blow our minds. Paul is calling us to walk in loving lowly service.

We think freedom means we can spend our day off any way we want to. Paul says freedom is to spend your day off looking after your neighbor's kids, so they can have some time to themselves. We think freedom is our right to enjoy the stuff from our own gardens. Paul says freedom is taking the stuff from our gardens over to the family that doesn't even have a garden. We think we are free to pursue our own portfolio, hobbies, resume, dreams, comforts. Paul says we are free to serve others from a heart of self-giving love. Wow!

Paul isn't just making this up. He's got a theological argument: the whole Old Testament Law has been fulfilled (is now already completed) by loving our neighbors.

He also has a practical argument. What happens when we walk alone or live as though we are the only one that matters? Two things: we indulge our own flesh (and by flesh Paul means our tendency to sin (more about the flesh in just a minute), and we end up at each other's throats—we bite, devour, and consume each other.

That's why Paul says to us: don't walk alone—walk in loving service.

Paul's pastor's heart isn't going to leave us hanging here. Now he's going to show us how we are to walk (vv. 16–26).

There are two options again here. We can walk by the Spirit or walk by the flesh.

To walk by the Spirit (v. 16), be led by the Spirit, (v. 18) or live by the Spirit (v. 25) means that we are submitting to the direction and power of the Holy Spirit in the lives we live and the choices we make. To walk by the flesh means we live our lives in submission to that pull within all of us to indulge in selfishness and sin.

We can't submit to both of these at the same time—they are opposed to each other. It's either/or not both/and. That means these two ways of walking are always at war within each of us—even when we have the Holy Spirit living within us. And it's not as though these two ways are equal either. Paul says in verse 24: "And those who belong to Christ Jesus have crucified the flesh with its passions and desires."

So, Paul says, "We don't have to sin anymore, but inexplicably, we still do. Sometimes we give in to our tendency to sin when we have the power to resist." For some reason the siren song of sin (the flesh) is very tempting to us.

I don't know how many of you have a weakness for country music, but for the sake of illustration, let's assume the sirens' song sounds more like a famous country singer. (Here I put on a cowboy hat, grab a guitar, sit on a stool, and try to give my best Johnny Cash imitation of "I Walk the Line.")

> Hello, I'm Johnny Flesh. This is a song about temptation:
> I'll make it very, very easy to transgress
> I'll make your life into an awful mess
> I'll wrap you up in cords of sin that bind
> If you cross that line, then you'll be mine.
>
> I'll tempt you just to think about yourself
> That you're OK and don't need anybody's help
> And promise you what you will never find
> If you cross that line, then you'll be mine.

Whether you like country music or not, we can all still be tempted to live selfishly when we know better. So, Paul takes the results of these two kinds of walking and puts them in sharp contrast to each other. Do you want to walk in the flesh? Here's where that leads: "Sexual immorality, impurity, sensuality, idolatry, sorcery, enmity, strife, jealousy, fits of anger, rivalries, dissensions, divisions, envy, drunkenness, orgies, and things like these" (vv.19b–21).

Did you notice how many of these "works of the flesh" have to do with how we relate to each other? Remember Paul is trying to keep the churches together because these false teachers are tearing them apart. A person who walks by the flesh will despise God and other people and be out of control.

Then, in contrast, Paul lists the fruit of the Spirit: "love, joy, peace, patience, kindness, goodness, faithfulness, gentleness, self-control" (vv. 22–23a).

Here's what we miss: we usually look at the fruit of the Spirit as evidence of the individual believer's maturity in their faith. But notice that Paul is more concerned here with these qualities that help us get along with others. It not just individual believers who should show the fruit of the Spirit but the whole church.

"Two Ways of Walking"

If we need more convincing, Paul interprets the fruit of the Spirit himself in verses 25 and 26: "If we live by the Spirit, let us also keep in step with the Spirit. Let us not become conceited, provoking one another, envying one another." Notice the interpersonal emphasis on these virtues. People who walk by the Spirit love God and each other and are not out of control.

So, Paul says here's how we are to walk: by the Spirit and not by the flesh.

Paul is still not satisfied until he shows us how this walking by the Spirit works itself out in actual situations—situations we find as we live together as part of the church. So, in the first ten verses of chapter 6, Paul tells us this is how we walk right here.

What Paul does is take a few different scenarios in the wider church and then he shows how we are supposed to respond. There are two ways of walking here too. They will become evident as we go along.

First—what happens when someone in the church gets caught up in sin? They need to be restored gently by those who are spiritually mature.

But notice, right in the midst of this, each of us is to make sure we don't get caught up in sin ourselves. There is no room for self-righteousness when we are walking by the Spirit.

Next—what happens when people in the church are weighed down with heavy burdens? We all need to bear each other's burdens; in doing so we are showing everything Jesus himself lived and taught.

But at the same time, we need to be careful about how we test our own work. There should be no freeloading off your neighbor when you have the capacity to pay your own way.

Third—and my favorite—what if the leaders in the congregation aren't being cared for sufficiently (v. 6)? Paul says you can't try to fool God and be cheap and expect to get away with it. We all will reap what we sow. There are consequences to our actions. If you don't think so, just ask Clarence.

Clarence Blethen played ball for the Boston Red Socks back in 1923. He had this bizarre habit of putting his false teeth in the back pocket of this uniform. He was trying to steal second base one day and ended up biting himself on the buttocks. The bleeding was so bad, he had to leave the game. I'm not sure what that proves other than if you try to steal something from someone else, you end up biting yourself you know where.

Besides, Paul says don't grow tired of caring for these leaders because there will be a time when you are rewarded if you don't give up.

By now you might have guessed the two ways of walking Paul is talking about here. One is sharing up and the other is giving up.

Again, Paul wants us to live our lives in such a way that we care for each other. These are immensely practical instructions. Paul wants us to be able to enjoy the unity God wants for his church. We can only do so by showing a gracious and generous spirit to each other and by walking the way Paul calls us to: walking in loving service; walking by the Spirit and by sharing up with each other.

This kind of walking can only be done together—with each other. This is the kind of walking that can't be done on our own. It's walking in rhythm with each other. it's a kind of walking that sounds a lot like dancing—or at least like walking to tasteful choreography if you were born like me: way too far to the right with two left feet.

Whatever you want to call it, Paul just wants to make sure we are in it together.

"This World Is Not Our Home"

1 John 2:12–17, ESV
October 8, 2017

Series Title: "Life. Light. Love."

PRAYER FOR ILLUMINATION

LORD, we are particularly thankful today, and we have every reason in the world to be so. We are thankful for all you have showered on us: this day, new life in Jesus, freedom to worship, this season of thanksgiving, and the privilege to share it with each other. Help this gratitude to find expression in our worship and our obedience to what you are calling us to do today. And may the words of my mouth and the meditations of all our hearts be pleasing in your sight, O LORD, our Rock and our Redeemer. Amen.

SERMON

Maybe you've seen one of those makeover shows on "reality" TV. It could be a person who needs some serious grooming and fashion advice or a dilapidated old house that needs major renovations. The point is always the same—we can hardly believe the difference between the "before" and the "after." The apostle John is one of those guys. When we first meet John, he's a self-centered, bad-tempered guy who is ready to call down fire on those who make him mad. He has a few anger management issues. Jesus gave him and his brother James a nickname: the sons of thunder. Pretty harmless but make a lot of noise. They were the noise boys—not lightning, just thunder—no zap, just yap.

Something has happened to this guy. When John writes these letters, he is known as the apostle of love. He writes more about love than any other biblical writer, and he also writes more about the world than anyone else. Doesn't that make you at least a bit curious about what he wants us to do?

It's been a while, so let me recap for a second. John is writing because some false teachers have been spreading heresy in the church, leaving the church but not leaving the believers alone. John has been reminding the believers of what they have in Christ, so they don't fall prey to this false teaching.

Now John is getting to end of the first part of this letter and so he wants to do a couple of things. The first is to remind us all of what he has said already—it's a review.

He is telling us the way it is.

For all the teachers in the crowd, John doesn't review by simply repeating himself over and over until our eyes glaze over. He finds a new way to say what he's already said.

He says it like it's poetry, or might I dare to say—a rap. Don't worry, I know I'm old and white and have no rhythm; we have a real rapper on staff now, so you can get the point without me having to embarrass myself—again.

What John does is address little children, fathers, and young men, then he does it again. There is nothing else like this in the rest of the letter. The commentators come to this section and go "what?" because most of them are old and white and have no rhythm either.

Here's what I think John is doing:

First, he talks to little children. This is how John talks about *all* of us as followers of Jesus—we see this all through the whole letter. And what is he saying to us? He is reminding us of two things: our sins have been forgiven and we know the Father; we know God. He wants us to remember what we have been given. These aren't gifts we're still hoping for, these are gifts we already have been given. John uses a verb tense here to show us these are things we have already.

Now that John has reminded all of us where we stand, he divides us further into fathers and young men.

Fathers are those of us, men and women, who have been around for quite a while and have known Jesus for a long time. They've seen it all and they bring stability to the rest of us. Look around the room today and you will see some of these people. They have served Jesus for a lifetime and they have a wealth of experience to share with the rest of us.

"This World Is Not Our Home"

If we're in the deep weeds and wonder if we'll ever come out of it, chances are, there is someone in this room who has been through something like that or worse before and can testify to the goodness of Christ through it all. Eugene Peterson, in *The Message*, calls these people "veterans." They have been through the war and know what it's like to walk in victory.

John also talks to young men—those just established in the faith but already full of fresh vigor and an enthusiasm that is contagious. John says to this group they have overcome the evil one; they are strong and have the word of God dwelling in them. These are great gifts, and these younger believers, both guys and girls, have a lot to offer as well. If John says the fathers bring stability, he's saying the younger ones bring vitality to the rest of us. They have energy and want to try new things. Peterson calls these believers "newcomers."

I've seen this work right here in our church staff. We are stronger as a staff because we have both older and younger pastors. They bring the energy and I bring the stability (sometimes). Together we are stronger. You can see that same thing happening all through our church if you are looking for it.

Notice that John celebrates these gifts among the church. Sometimes we're not so sure. We might see these gifts as barriers. The older among us might look our noses down at the younger and say they are just flighty and have no self-discipline. They have attention spans shorter than goldfish and are addicted to their screens. The younger among us might look at the older and say they are just crotchety and grumpy and couldn't change to save their lives.

Some of this may even be true, but it's a "glass-half-empty" perspective. John calls us to see that we are part of the same family, and we all bring strengths to the table.

This is how he reminds us of what he been telling us up to this point. He's told us the way it is. Now he's going to tell us the way it should be.

John gives ten commands in this letter and waits until now to give us his first one. In the book of James, a letter of about the same length, there are fifty-five commands. This is John's first command: "Do not love the world or the things of the world. If anyone loves the world, the love of the Father is not in him" (1 John 2:15).

You might be saying, "Wait a minute—doesn't it say that God loved the world—John 3:16?" You're right, God does love the world, but . . .a couple of things: 1) you *ain't* God, and 2) when God loves the world he shows it by giving his Son to save it. When we love the world, we don't give anything, we take stuff, we want stuff.

John says we need to make a choice here. Either we love God or we love the world, and we can't do both. These are hard words to hear in our times. We are people of the both/and, not people of the either/or. But John is an either/or kind of guy. He does this same kind of contrasting all through his writings. He contrasts light and darkness, life and death, love and hate, above and below, truth and falsehood, belief and unbelief, and eternal and temporary. That's a lot of contrasting.

We see it's a matter of either/or in all these contrasts. Not because they are equally as strong (in John's mind the one side is stronger than the other), but because they still are opposed to each other.

The main contrast here is between the Father and the world. Either we love the Father (God) or we love the world. Either we long for what the Father gives us (like John has just told us in vv. 12–14), or we long for what the world can give us. When John is talking about the world here, he's talking about the whole system and way of life that is organized against what God wants.

John knows we would like to have it both ways—to love God but also enjoy the perks that come from living in the world. Kind of the same way moths are attracted to the flame. But John knows the danger of divided loyalties and so he does us the favor of giving two very good reasons why we shouldn't love the world.

The first reason is found in verse 16: "For all that is in the world—the desires of the flesh and the desires of the eyes and pride in possessions—is not from the Father but is from the world."

Love of the world is summed up in these three phrases: the desires of the flesh, the desires of the eyes, and pride in possessions. Some have tried to make parallels here with Eve in the garden of Eden when she saw the forbidden fruit or with Jesus when he was tempted by Satan in the wilderness. That's probably trying to force the parallels a bit too far, even though it's "tempting" to do so.

John is giving a picture of what the world dangles in front of us. The desires of the flesh are any desire or longing for something that draws us away from God. It's the longing for what is not good for us. This can happen to any of us. We know deep down it is not good for us, but it can still keep calling our name until we give in—whether that is a second piece of chocolate cake, a certain relationship, a certain group of friends, a certain website, a particular job or contract—it doesn't matter. If it keeps us away from loving God with all our heart, soul, mind and strength; it is a desire of the flesh.

The desires of the eyes are the longings for those things that look so good on the outside that we don't bother asking what they might be hiding on the inside. That's why every car in the used car lot is washed and polished to a shine; that's why there are all kinds of tempting things within easy reach in the grocery checkout; that's why Facebook posts make you look like a million bucks. It's a façade. All you need to do is visit the set of a TV show to know what John is talking about. What looks good on camera is actually just fake, flimsy props made out of plywood and cardboard.

The third of these is the pride of possessions. This is putting our confidence in what we have and what we do. It's the accumulation of property and experiences that makes us feel better than other people. Someone has a new car, we scoff because our new car is more luxurious than theirs. Somebody goes on a vacation to BC and we don't care because we have a timeshare in Hawaii. There is a popular saying: he who dies with the most toys wins. John is saying: he who dies with the most toys dies. All these desires take us further from God and more into ourselves. John says it's not a both/and, it's an either/or.

The second reason for not loving the world is in verse 17: "And the world is passing away along with its desires, but whoever does the will of God abides forever." Just in case we think John doesn't want us to enjoy life at all, he points out something important. These desires that appear so important at the time are only temporary; they do not satisfy, and they will be gone before you know it. Elvis might have been buried in a Cadillac, but he still was buried—and rumors of his resurrection are highly exaggerated.

In the end, it all boils down to this: love the one who gives you life. Don't waste your life longing for things that will just take you away from God and won't last. Don't sell out for the big paycheck or the trophy spouse or the big house. John is warning us for our own good. He's doing the same thing they did in the Dutch town of Barneveld. They noticed the children playing with a metal object in the playground and realized it was an unexploded artillery shell. Much to the dismay of the children, they took it away and had it detonated in a secure place. John is trying to keep us from this kind of situation. We might enjoy what the world offers. We might even be having a blast. but John, in his own loving way, reminds us "the blast won't last!" The only thing that will last forever is our relationship with our heavenly Father who loved us even when we didn't want him to.

"It's All in the Family"

1 John 3:11–24, ESV
October 29, 2017

Series Title: "Life. Light. Love"

PRAYER FOR ILLUMINATION

LORD, we can hardly believe how blessed we are to be your children. Forgive us for those times when we are not completely blown away by this fact. Help us in those moments when we struggle to get our minds around the reality of your love for us. Help us to remember our security rests in you and not in ourselves. And may the words of my mouth and the meditations of all our hearts be pleasing in your sight, O LORD, our Rock and our Redeemer. Amen.

SERMON

If we hear something long enough, even if it isn't true, we can begin to believe it. Maybe you've grown up with someone who has called you dumb or ugly. Maybe you've been told you would never amount to anything or that you can't cut it. Or, in the opposite extreme, maybe you've been told you can do anything you set your mind to, so you try to leap over tall buildings and fall flat on your face.

These constant messages can mess with our heads and can distort reality for us. Sometimes perception becomes reality and we find ourselves living out these life scripts—even if they may not be true.

I grew up on a farm. I had a brother and a sister. When there are two boys on the family farm, usually one is chosen to keep the farm in the

"It's All in the Family"

family and the other is chosen to leave. I know my father wasn't trying to be mean, but it was very obvious that he didn't think I was farmer material. I kept breaking stuff by accident. Now, my brother, who kept breaking stuff on purpose, apparently was farmer material. It didn't take long for me to realize I was not the handy or mechanically-minded one, so I needed to consider another line of work. My Dad used to say if I couldn't make my living with my hands, I could always make a living with my wits—after all, half a living is better than nothing! He was kidding, I think.

This life script has stuck with me all my life. When we first moved to Caronport over fifteen years ago, I needed to borrow a rototiller to till up our garden. One of my new neighbors who will remain nameless, says, "I know you were born on a farm, so you can use my rototiller." Big mistake. Did you know rototillers can climb trees?

This is what is happening in the letter of 1 John. False teachers have been messing with the minds of the believers there—even after these scoundrels have left the church. These heretics have been hammering away at these Christians, saying they are second-rate and that they really don't know God. This is starting to erode their confidence some. One of John's aims in this letter is to reassure the believers there.

These believers are experiencing a crisis of confidence. Are we really saved? How do we know we belong to God? Maybe these false teachers are right about us. So, John says in 2:28: "And now, little children, abide in him, so that when he appears we may have confidence and not shrink from him in shame at his coming."

John started with us last week when Pastor Josh reminded us we are God's children and our identity doesn't rest in our achievements. And John continues this morning, giving us three more assurances of who we are as children of God. These three are so intertwined that it's impossible to separate them.

John begins by reminding us we have confidence because we have obeyed the call to love each other (vv. 11–18).

He starts by saying, "For [linking back to what he has just said about us being God's children] this is the message that you have heard from the beginning, that we should love one another" (1 John 3:11).

Notice what John is saying here. He's not saying we can earn our own confidence before God by loving each other. He's saying our assurance is shown by the fact that we do love each other.

This is the first time John mentions this love for each other, so he's going to spend some time showing us what he means by it.

He begins with a negative example: here's how not to love each other. Look at Cain. Remember Cain? Adam and Eve, our most ancient ancestors had two boys: Cain and Abel. Cain was a farmer and Abel was a shepherd. Cain raised plants and Abel raised sheep. We're not sure what went wrong with Cain, but he did something to displease God. Maybe he wanted to raise sheep, but he wasn't Abel. Anyway, he ends up murdering his brother—literally "butchering" him.

John points at Cain and says, "Don't do this because Cain represents those who are empowered by Satan and what I call 'the world.'" Cain didn't love his brother, he hated him, and ended up murdering him. John makes this connection: those who hate others, especially those close to them, are murderers. Everyone knows that murderers don't have eternal life. So that's John's negative argument.

But that's not enough for John—he turns the negative on its ear and gives us the positive side.

Verse 16: "By this we know love, that he laid down his life for us, and we ought to lay down our lives for our brothers."

The positive example, which should be no surprise, is Jesus. Hatred leads us to take things away from others and give it to ourselves. Love lays down what we have and gives it to others. Hatred is self-focused; love is other-focused.

Jesus is our example, and here's how it might work for us—here's a way we can lay down what belongs to us and give it to others. "But if anyone has the world's goods and sees his brother in need, yet closes his heart against him, how does God's love abide in him?" (v. 17).

Let's not miss this: our confidence before God is a result of how natural it is for us to reach out and help each other when we see others in need. Last week, Pastor Josh said we have confidence because we are God's children and then he announced he and Dochelle are adopting a child. That's a hard act to follow.

This is why we are encouraged to love each other, to love our neighbors. We show our love to others by giving what is ours to them. Who could be more in need than a college student, right? So here are two gift cards, buy something you need. And if you have enough money, give it to a classmate or a roommate. [Pass out two gifts cards to two college students.]

"It's All in the Family"

We are assured that we belong to Jesus as we act like Jesus. Jesus acted for the good of others—so should we. It's not rocket science—it's God math.

That's why John gives us these two bridge verses in 18 and 19: "Little children, let us not love in word or talk, but in deed and in truth. By this we shall know that we are of the truth and reassure our hearts before him." He's leading us to our next assurance.

Not only are we confident by obeying the command to love each other, we also are confident because of our trust in Christ (vv. 19-24).

Look at verses 21–23: "Beloved, if our heart does not condemn us, we have confidence before God; and whatever we ask we receive from him, because we keep his commandments and do what pleases him. *and this is his commandment, that we believe in the name of his son Jesus Christ and love one another*, just as he has commanded us" (emphasis added).

These two always go together—belief (trust) and obedience. And what we need to remember is both are pointing away from ourselves, not toward us. Belief is not important because it's us who is believing. Belief is important because of who we believe in—the object of our belief, not us as the subject of believing. Obedience is necessary not because it is us who is obeying—but because of whom we obey.

If our belief and obedience depend on us, we're hooped. When we're feeling up, we're up. But when we're down, we have this crisis of confidence again. Our lives are like rollercoasters, complete with the nausea. That's why John says in verse 20: "For whenever our heart condemns us, God is greater than our heart, and he knows everything."

Our confidence or assurance before God does not depend on us, but on God. When our confidence falters, God stands fast. When we are weak, he is strong. When we wobble like a bobble head, God never does—his love for us never fails.

Sometimes we get ourselves into way too much trouble just because we think too much depends on us. That's a dead-end street.

Even when little kids get into trouble in the playground, they don't try to put it all on themselves. They say, "Wait 'til I tell my big brother," or, "Wait 'til I tell my Dad!" When did we forget this?

John isn't done with us yet. Our confidence doesn't just come from our obedience to the call to love each other but also because of the gift of the Holy Spirit. Verse 24: "Whoever keeps his commandments abides in God and God in him. *and by this we know that he abides in us, by the Spirit whom he has given us*" (emphasis added).

John doesn't say very much about the Holy Spirit in this letter. Maybe he thinks we already know about his ministry in our lives. Maybe he assumes we've all read his Gospel or heard the words of Paul to the Romans: "The Spirit himself bears witness with our spirit that we are children of God" (8:16).

What he does say is the Spirit is a gift to us. So again, the emphasis is on the One who gives the gift—God.

John has been reassuring us when we wonder if we still belong to God. He comes alongside us, puts his arm around us, and assures us of the confidence we can have as children of God.

If there is one common denominator that ties all three of these assurances together, it's that they're not about us, about who we think we are, or how we are feeling at any given moment. Our confidence is found not in ourselves but in God.

The command to love takes us beyond our care for ourselves to caring for others.

Our believing is based on the God who knows everything, not on our hearts which tend to leave us twisting in the wind at times.

The Holy Spirit is a gift from God. All these assurances take the spotlight off us and put it on God.

If John could take all this and state it in the negative, he'd say: the greatest enemy of our confidence before God is our self-consciousness. So, the secret to our confidence is a God-focus and self-forgetfulness.

Years ago, when my son Nathan turned four, I thought it was high time he learned to play hockey. I bought him all the gear and signed him up to play in Pownal, Prince Edward Island. He could barely even stand on his skates. I told him not to worry and just skate around the outside of the rink. Then when the coach blew the whistle to turn around, I told him skate the other way.

I plunked him on the ice and went to join all the other doting parents. They were all saying, "Look at that fast one. That's my boy," and "See that one bigger than all the rest? That's my girl!" As I looked out, I noticed everyone was skating the same way except for one kid—you guessed it. So, I thought to myself, "The coach is going to blow the whistle and soon they'll all be skating the same way." He blew the whistle, and everyone, including Nathan turned around. Then it struck me—my son may not be the best skater in the world, but he does not follow the crowd, he leads it. So, there

I was, hanging over the boards from the waist, pointing at my son and saying, "That's my boy!"

Our sense of confidence before God is not up to us, what we do or how we are feeling at the moment. Our confidence comes from the fact that we are loved by God. That will not change because we are God's children, and he lives in us. And because he lives in us, we can live for each other.

We are different because we are family. And as family members, we love each other and serve each other. We don't beat on each other, we brag on each other. We do this not because we're better than everyone else. We do it because God lives in us and gives us the confidence to act like his children. And when we act like his children, God hangs over the boards of heaven from the waist, points at us and says, "Hey, look! There's my kids!"

"A Dream of Irresistible Influence"

Matthew 5:13–16, ESV
April 15, 2018

Series Title: "The King's Speech"

PRAYER FOR ILLUMINATION

LORD, we want to see ourselves as part of the crowd scattered all over the green hills of Galilee as you speak to us about living in your kingdom. Open our ears to hear what we might not have heard before. Remind us of who we are and what you would have us do. Give us a glimpse of your kingdom and help us see what you can see. And may the words of my mouth and the meditations of all our hearts be pleasing in your sight, O LORD, our Rock and our Redeemer. Amen.

SERMON

I'm holding in my hand, something you may not have seen before—a Jesus action figure.

I got it at a dollar store in Moose Jaw. I saw it there on the shelf and a hundred sermon illustrations crossed my mind, so I bought it—even though it might be breaking the second commandment about graven images—even plastic ones. We have to ask ourselves, "Why would anyone buy something like this?" And the answer is, "Everyone can use a little Jesus!" That's true in a number of ways. You can use a little Jesus because you're in control. He's safely encased in plastic, so he can't get out and do any damage—like overturning the tables of money changers, cursing fig trees, or telling us what to do. We can all use a little Jesus. A little Jesus is a safe Jesus. A little Jesus doesn't make any demands on us. He fits right into our pockets and we can take him out and put him back whenever we want to.

People don't mind it as long we have a little Jesus because they don't like it when we get all "weird" and "religious" on them. So, a little Jesus can come in downright handy.

Until, that is, we open the Bible and read the Sermon on the Mount in Matthew chapters 5–7. No little Jesus here. He looks more like this: [Project an image of Christ the Redeemer statue above Rio de Janeiro.]

And even this doesn't do justice to the real Jesus.

In these chapters in Matthew's Gospel, we see a big Jesus and this big Jesus is telling us what life can be like if we follow him as his disciples. He's not trying to make it impossible for us. He's not saying, "This kind of life can only happen during the millennium," or it's a short-term spiritual boot camp that will prepare us for his soon return. Jesus is saying, "This is what life can be like if we truly seek first his kingdom, if we follow him completely." This is Jesus' dream for us—this Sermon on the Mount is his messianic imagination at work. This is not Jesus trying to act like a new lawmaker. This is Jesus the divine dreamer—calling us to dream with him about what life could be like if we treat him like a big Jesus.

Last week Pastor Josh introduced Jesus' sermon and showed us what we are to be like if we want to be part of this kingdom dream. And what Jesus says today falls right in line with where he left off last week.

Jesus is going to get to the part about what we're supposed to do—but he doesn't start there. He starts by telling us what we *are*.

Jesus uses these two phrases: he says, "You are the salt of the earth and the light of the world." We are salt and light. What does he mean?

Salt had many uses back in Jesus' time. They used salt as money (soldiers used to get paid in salt—if they were worth their salt); it was a preservative, used as fertilizer (in small doses), a disinfectant, and a spice to flavor their food. That's a lot of uses. People often try to figure out which of these uses Jesus is thinking about when he talks about us being salt. I think it's much simpler than that. People in Jesus' day couldn't imagine life without salt. It added so much to life in so many ways. And this is Jesus' point: we're like salt, to make life better, to make such an impact and be such an influence that we make life better.

Notice Jesus says you *are* the salt of the earth—not you could be or should be or one day you might be. You *are*. This is a statement of fact. This is what God has made us.

What do you think of when you think of salt? You think of saltiness. It's inconceivable to think of salt that isn't salty. Sodium chloride is always salty—it's a stable compound so it's always supposed to be salty. And what do you call salt that isn't salty? Pavement!

The way salt can lose its saltiness is through impurities. I was just floating in the Dead Sea a couple months ago. I can float there because of the high salt content in the water—but it's not pure salt—it's mostly sludge and black slime. I would not want to shake that stuff on my French fries because it's too impure. (And besides, it would look too much like poutine.)

If the whole salt thing doesn't make sense to you, Jesus goes on to call us light. Light shows the way, dispels the darkness, and brings healing. Again, this is what we are. We have been designed by God to bring light; that is what light does.

Again, Jesus says that light that is hidden is a contradiction in terms. You can't hide a city's lights when it's built on a hill. We can see Regina's lights at night, and it's on land that is flat as a pancake. You don't take a lamp and hide it under a pail. You put it on a stand—that way it can do what it's designed to do: shine! When we were in Israel, one of our hosts gave me a little replica lamp like the ones they used back in Jesus' time. You pour the oil in and the wick sticks out so you can light it and the lamp can shine. [Demonstrate with little clay lamp.]

Jesus is making the same point: he has made us salt and light. It is to be our very nature to be salty and bright. We are to have this kind of positive influence on our surroundings.

If we listen carefully to what Jesus is saying, not only do we hear him tell us what we are—we are salt and light, so shine—but he also tells us who we do it for.

Jesus calls us "the salt *of the earth*" and "the light *of the world*." He says a light "gives light *to all in the room*." He also says, "Let your light shine *before others*." Do you see the common theme? We are salty and bright for the benefit of others. Jesus isn't talking about other nice church people like us, he's talking about people who don't know or follow Jesus, people who don't know that Jesus has come to give them a brand-new life that they could never gain on their own. People who don't know that without Jesus they are hooped and doomed to mess up their lives by their own selfishness and sin.

"A Dream of Irresistible Influence"

Jesus isn't calling us inward—to circle the wagons and just treat each other with special kindness. Jesus is calling us outward. Jesus' dream is that his people will lead the way in being a positive influence on the entire world. This is what it means to be Jesus' follower, to be his disciple, to dream Jesus' dream along with him.

This is what Jesus is up to because he knows where it will lead. So, he takes the time to show us we are indeed salt and light and then he tells us why we are. Verse 16: "In the same way, let your light shine before others, *so that* they may see your good works and give glory to your Father who is in heaven."

Being salt and light is not just a matter of showing up and looking salty or bright. Being salt and light is about what we do. Jesus says people are to see our good works. In other words, being salt and light means we are actively doing things that bring great benefit to the whole world. Jesus can't picture us any other way. Followers of Jesus who are not out there influencing the world by what they are doing are like "saltless" salt or dark light. We have been saved to serve; what we do does make a difference. To be salt and light isn't talking about our *status*, it's about our *function*—what we have been called to do. How can we be followers of Jesus and not do what he has made us to do?

And why do we do what we do? So that others will see our good works—so they will notice the difference God's kingdom actions make and then they will give glory to God.

We're not salty by just huddling together, wringing our hands, and complaining how unchristian the non-Christians are, or how bad the government is and how hard it is to be a Christian in our world. We are salty by allowing our actions to be redemptive—showing the love of Christ as we work in our communities and with our neighbors, our schools, businesses, and governments. Our work is our witness.

A huge part of Jesus' dream for his kingdom is to have us actively working to bring positive, irresistible influence to the world—to the world right around us and the world beyond us. This is who we are—salt and light. And when we show the world who we are, the world will see who God is.

Let's be real—this is not going to happen if all we have is a little Jesus. But that can happen when we realize we can't *use* a big Jesus—we *obey* a big Jesus. If we take Jesus seriously, amazing things can happen.

A couple of decades ago, Robert Lewis, the pastor of a megachurch in Little Rock, Arkansas, started to ask the question, "If our church disappeared, would our community even notice we were gone?" They went to the mayor and asked if there was anything they could do, and they got a list. The difference they made in their city was so astounding that the mayor started coming to *them*.

LifeBridge Christian Church in Longmont, Colorado did much the same. They started on a journey that led them to become a neighboring church and the book they wrote has started a gentle revolution right here in Caronport.

Every year in Steinbach, Manitoba, 1,400 volunteers from the churches are given yellow T-shirts; they cover the entire town and pick up all the garbage. They look like an army of dandelions. This is how they show their faith.

What happens when we are salt and light—when our good works are undeniable and irresistible? People notice, and they are amazed. God is honored, and his kingdom comes—bit by bit.

If we don't get what Jesus is saying, we won't get the rest of the Sermon on the Mount. Jesus is saying who we are shines through what we do.

This is Jesus' "I Have a Dream speech." Jesus stands on the side of this mountain and says,

> I have a dream today.
> I have a dream that every disciple will not be judged by what he says but by what he does.
> I have a dream that every disciple will reach out to her neighbor in love and self-sacrifice.
> I have a dream today!
> I have a dream that the whole world will stand in wordless wonder as they see my disciples in action.
> I have a dream where my disciples will be known for their hospitality and not their hypocrisy.
> I have a dream that my Father's will be done on earth as it is in heaven.
> I have a dream today!

That's a big dream—but he's a big Jesus. How big is your Jesus?

"A Dream of Real Righteousness"

Matthew 5:17–20, ESV
April 22, 2018

Series Title: "The King's Speech"

PRAYER FOR ILLUMINATION

LORD, we know you are good—always have been, always will be. We've always been on the receiving end of your goodness, and we would be lost without it. We desperately want to reflect your goodness, but we are easily confused and deceived. Show us what you want us to be and how we get there. And may the words of my mouth and the meditations of all our hearts be pleasing in your sight, O LORD, our Rock and our Redeemer. Amen.

SERMON

There are some big questions we need to ask ourselves at some point: Who are we? Why are we here? How did we get this way? How do we fix that? Where are we heading? One of these big questions is: What is it about us that makes us truly right or good? What makes us what God wants us to be? To use biblical terminology, what makes us righteous, acceptable to God? Then we want to know if we can do this ourselves. Some might say we can, because especially now, we have all kinds of gadgets that can help us get better. Maybe you've heard of smartphones or smartwatches—now you can buy a smart fork that measures how fast you eat and warns you when you aren't chewing enough. For fifty dollars you can buy a smart toothbrush that connects with an app on your phone. You can buy software called PostureTrack® that tells you when you are slouching, or you can get a feature installed in your car that chirps at you whenever you are driving carelessly (if you haven't married someone who will do that for free). Even with all these gadgets, we know something is missing.

In these next few weeks, Jesus sets out to answer this question about how we can be good people.

Remember what we have in his Sermon on the Mount is his vision for the kingdom of heaven, of what life can be like if all his followers seek first his kingdom and his righteousness. It's his messianic imagination at work and he calls us to be part of this dream—a big dream made by a big Jesus.

So, Jesus introduces us to two different ways to get right with God, to be right and good people. There is the way of the scribes and Pharisees, the spiritual leaders of his own day, and then there is his way, the Jesus way.

These are opposing views, but they both agree on one thing. They agree that our "rightness" comes from what God wants for us. What God wants for us is called the Law. What God wants for us hasn't changed. *How we receive what God wants for us* is what makes the difference.

On the one hand you have God's people, Israel. God gave them his gift of Law to help them be what he wanted them to be—a light to all the other nations. The problem is they never seemed to live up to this gift. They messed up in the wilderness, they messed up in the promised land, and they ended up in captivity. By the time Jesus arrives on the scene, the spiritual leaders seem to have lost their calling to be the light and had settled for simply managing sin. They took God's Law and widened it (stretched it out) so they could have a rule for every possible situation (kind of like Hallmark cards).

So, they had hundreds of rules about how to observe Sabbath and what to eat and how to prepare it.

Then on the other hand, Jesus comes along and doesn't seem to share their love of rules and does things on the Sabbath that drives these leaders crazy. And Jesus hangs out with people the scribes and Pharisees had written off as unclean. It doesn't take long for the word to get out that this Jesus isn't playing by the rules; he's playing fast and loose with the Law of God.

So here is where Jesus takes time to spell out what being right and good is to look like in the kingdom of heaven—in his big dream for us all.

He begins with himself in verses 17 and 18 where he says he (Jesus) fully fills the law.

"A Dream of Real Righteousness"

"Do not think I have come to abolish the Law and the Prophets (the Old Testament); I have not come to abolish them but to fulfill them. For truly I say to you, until heaven and earth pass away, not an iota, not a dot, will pass from the Law until all is accomplished."

Jesus hasn't come to *widen or stretch* what God wants us to be and do (the Law), nor has he come to *promote* it or *completely abolish or rub it out*—he has come (this is his purpose, this is why he came), he has come to *fulfill* the Law.

OK, what does that mean? You can't read Matthew's Gospel without running into this phrase over and over: "This was done to fulfill what the prophets said." Jesus is able to fulfill everything Israel couldn't. Israel failed while being tested in the wilderness—Jesus didn't. Israel kept being unfaithful to God—Jesus was always faithful.

Everything Jesus does is a fulfilling of what God expected and what Israel failed to do.

To fulfill literally means to fully fill. It's like me taking a pitcher of water and slowly filling a glass until it is full and overflows. [I then demonstrate this by filling a glass of water until it overflows.] Israel is running on empty and they needed someone to fill things fully. In the midst of their failure, they would cry out for the day when Messiah would come and fill things fully. They would say, "We are weak and worship other gods—but when Messiah comes, true worship will fill the earth. We sin against each other and oppress each other, but when Messiah comes, the earth will be filled with righteousness and peace."

It's a bit like Narnia when Lucy first visits it from the wardrobe. It's always winter, but never Christmas. Life is bleak, but Mr. Beaver is still hopeful as he says, "Wrong will be right, when Aslan comes in sight."

"When Messiah comes . . .": so now in Jesus the Messiah has come, and in what he says and what he does, he brings fullness to the Law. He doesn't abolish it completely or even try to stretch it like the scribes and Pharisees did. He himself is the fulfilling of what God wants for us.

God has always wanted us to love and worship him. Jesus is the way, the truth, and the life and no one comes to the Father except through him. God has always wanted us to be holy. Jesus embodies what it means to be holy. God has always wanted us to treat each other well. Jesus shows us what true love is.

There were laws about observing Sabbath. Jesus comes and says he is the Lord of the Sabbath. There were laws about what foods made you unclean or unholy. Jesus says that it isn't what goes into you that makes you unholy, it's what comes out of you.

Jesus comes to fully fill the Law, not abolish it. Nor does he come to widen or stretch the Law like the religious scribes and Pharisees. Jesus actually comes to deepen the Law, to internalize it. So, the Law is not going to disappear—not even the smallest part of it—but all of it is fully filled in Jesus.

So, Jesus fulfills the Law by fully filling it.

Now that's the part about Jesus and how *he* wants us to be the kind of good and right person we should be. What about us and our part? Does Jesus have anything to say about us?

Glad you asked because yes, he does. He goes on in verses 19 and 20:

> Therefore whoever relaxes one of the least of these commandments and teaches others to do the same will be called least in the kingdom of heaven, but whoever does them and teaches them will be called great in the kingdom of heaven. For I tell you, unless your righteousness exceeds that of the scribes and Pharisees, you will never enter the kingdom of heaven.

Since Jesus has fully filled the Law, now we are to fully follow Jesus.

We need to follow what Jesus is saying here or we'll get really confused. This second part of Jesus' argument is based on the first part and if we don't get that, we'll end up in worse shape than the scribes and Pharisees who were killing themselves trying to keep all the rules they made to stretch out the Law.

Jesus starts with this word "therefore"—in other words what he's saying now is based on what he's just told us. He just told us he was fully filling the Law—he was the one who could really tell us what God wants for and from us.

So, if it is Jesus who can tell us what God wants, we aren't free to pick and choose what parts we'll obey and what parts we won't. Nor are we free to be like the scribes and Pharisees who added to the Law to stretch it out.

That is not the way it works in the kingdom of heaven—Jesus' big dream for how life is going to be when he is in control. That puts us on the outside looking in.

Jesus is looking for something better from us than the rule-keeping of the scribes and Pharisees. He wants our righteousness to exceed that. He wants our righteousness to be deeper than that. He wants us to act like he

"A Dream of Real Righteousness"

wants us to because it comes from within us—because we want to do it that way, not because we have to do it that way.

This is what Dallas Willard calls a "kingdom heart." If we want to be part of this kingdom of heaven, to be part of Jesus' big dream for his world, we are to follow Jesus fully from our hearts, from our kingdom hearts.

That means it's not enough to just smile nicely and walk right by when we see someone who is obviously having a rough time. We will want to go over to that person and see if there is something we could do to help. Not because we have to but because we have a kingdom heart to help.

Or if we see someone pulled off the side of the road with a flat tire, it's not enough to give them lots of room as you drive past just so you don't spray gravel or dust all over them. We pull over and see if we can give a hand—not because we're handy or feel guilty but because we have a kingdom heart that wants to help.

Maybe this is starting to make a little sense, but you may want a few more examples before it sinks in. Well, Jesus has thought of that too and we'll be spending the next few weeks unpacking the six examples Jesus gives of what he's talking about here. That will take us to the end of the fifth chapter of Matthew's Gospel. By the time we're done with these examples, we should have a pretty good picture of what it means to act out of a kingdom heart.

This is Jesus' big dream for us. This is how he wants us to act—out of kingdom hearts overflowing with love for the other person. This is how we show that we are right and good people—Jesus' kind of people.

What Jesus is saying is: find your "rightness" in Jesus' fullness.

This is Jesus' dream for us. And the thing is, Jesus dreams big dreams, but not impossible ones.

"A Dream of Intentional Obedience"

Matthew 7:24–29, ESV
July 15, 2018

Series Title: "The King's Speech"

PRAYER FOR ILLUMINATION

LORD, we come to you because we've come to the end of ourselves and we know you alone are mighty to save. You alone have shown us the power of grace and the paths of grace. We can trust you like no other. Meet us here today, in the midst of our joys and sorrows, our to-do lists and our wish lists, and lead us in the way everlasting. So, may the words of my mouth and the mediations of all our hearts be pleasing in your sight, O LORD, our Rock and our Redeemer. Amen.

SERMON

Have you ever been visiting a different church and you're not sure how to act—whether this is an "*AAA*men" church of an "*AWE*men" church? Do you eat and drink the Communion elements right when they're passed, or do you wait and then eat and drink together? When do we sit down and when do we stand up? This standing up and sitting down stuff can get confusing. When Jesus starts preaching this sermon, back at the beginning of Matthew chapter 5, he sits down; when he's done, he stands up and goes back down the mountain. Today I stand up when I preach and then I will sit down when I'm done—probably much later than you would have liked. This is all very confusing, isn't it?

"A Dream of Intentional Obedience"

We can see Jesus isn't confused, he knows exactly what he's doing. Right about now he's getting ready to stand up, to finish his sermon. Along with everything else, Jesus is the master preacher.

Time out for a quick preaching lesson: Every sermon has three parts, an introduction, the body of the sermon, and the conclusion. It's like riding on a plane: the takeoff, the flight, and the landing. The introduction, like the takeoff, should be short. If you take too long to take off, you run out of runway. The flight takes the longest because that's when we are fed (much better than a glass of water and some pretzels that you get on most domestic flights these days). The sermon isn't over until you land the plane. You need to land on purpose. You don't just stop in mid-air, nor should you circle the airport until you run out of gas. The landing is the most critical part of the flight.

Today we see Jesus landing the plane—he's getting ready to stand up. He started the landing back in verse 13 and now he's in the final approach. Every flight when you can land the plane and stand up and walk away is a good flight.

Jesus introduced his sermon back in chapter 5: "Seeing the crowds, he went up on the mountain, and when he sat down, his disciples came to him. And he opened his mouth and taught them." Everything after that has been the sermon itself; now Jesus is ready to wrap it up and stand up and walk away. This is the most critical part of the sermon. If we miss this, we miss it all.

When some preachers conclude, they get all red in the face, shake a boney finger in your face, and make some kind of idle threat that doesn't work very well. What does Jesus do? He tells two little stories about two different guys. One of these two is wise and the other is not.

Jesus' two stories are about home construction—which seems like an odd way to end a sermon.

The first guy decides to build his house on a firm foundation, so he builds his house on bedrock. In Luke's version of this same story, Jesus says he "dug deep and laid the foundation on the rock." What does *that* mean?

If you ask anyone who builds houses, they will tell you how important it is to build on a solid foundation. Forget everything you heard about the three little pigs and what their houses were made of. You can have a great looking house, but if the foundation is bad, it will not stand the test of time.

That's why Jesus says, "the rain fell, and the floods came, and the winds blew and beat on that house." Israel is a dry country, with very little rainfall. But in the fall season, rains can come with a vengeance. The dry valleys are suddenly flooded, and everything greens up. You want to be ready when this comes. You don't want to be tenting out in a valley when the rains come.

Is Jesus telling us a firm foundation will help us when we experience the storms of life? When life is the hardest and we're hit by one flood after another? While that is true, I don't think that is Jesus' main point. He's pointing ultimately to the final judgement. Jesus isn't so much talking about how he will help us through the tough times—he will, but this is not the text that teaches us that. Jesus is talking about what makes us real followers of his, and we will never know for sure until the end. A truly good house is one that still stands. We don't know much about that out here. But all we need to do is visit a part of the world that has been building houses for centuries and millennia, and we get a better sense of the stability Jesus is talking about.

Jesus says what makes this house last is that it is founded on the rock. Real estate agents say the most important part of a house is location, location, location. Jesus says it's foundation, foundation, foundation.

It's tempting to say he built it on the rock, which means he built his life on Jesus. Like the old chorus about the wise man building his house upon the rock and the foolish man building his house upon the sand, which ends with the line: "So build your house on the Lord." It's tempting, but wrong. What Jesus is talking about here is what he has just said throughout his Sermon on the Mount. If our lives reflect what Jesus has been teaching us, our lives will stand up to the ultimate test of judgment.

This is what Jesus means when he talks about building on a firm foundation. He describes wise builders as "everyone then who hears these words of mine and *does them*."

Then Jesus tells us about the other guy—the guy who is not so bright but too dumb to know it, the guy who thinks he knows better than everyone when he doesn't, the guy who thinks oceanfront property means building his house right on the beach. We already know that's not going to work, don't we? Jesus is setting us up.

I went to great lengths to prove this—I went all the way to Prince Edward Island to show to myself, once and for all, that building on sand is dumb. I went out on the beach and dug a hole, but the sides kept caving in. Sand is not a firm foundation.

Maybe you've been to Italy and seen the Leaning Tower, or maybe you have been paying attention as you drive into Moose Jaw and see that house to the north of the highway that sits on a slant.

"A Dream of Intentional Obedience"

The thing is, you can have a pretty good-looking house out on the sand until the rains come, or the tide comes in. Then we see what happens. Jesus says not only does that house fall down, but its collapse is spectacular. Maybe you saw footage of the demolition of the old Mosaic Stadium. That was a rather spectacular falling. Like the words of that same old chorus: "and the house on the sand went *splat*!"

Without us even noticing, Jesus has delivered a serious warning. We are still saying to ourselves, "That silly moron—who would build a house on sand anyway?"

Then we remember how Jesus describes those foolish ones: "And everyone who hears these words of mine and *does not do them*." Suddenly it gets a lot more pointed and personal. How many of us have known what Jesus has told us to do and haven't done it? Do we need a show of hands?

And . . . that's it. Jesus is done. He stands up and walks down the hill, leaving us with our mouths hanging open.

If we've been paying attention, we've learned something else about sermons—at least the good ones. The sermon isn't over just because the preacher has stopped preaching. The sermon isn't over until we respond to it—until it takes root in our actions and attitudes.

What happens after Jesus is done with his sermon? "And when Jesus finished these sayings [this is how Matthew signals that the teaching time is over—he does this another four times in his Gospel], the crowds were astonished at his teaching, for he was teaching them as one who had authority, and not as their scribes."

So, we think, that's good, right? They were astonished, blown away. Most preachers secretly wish this was the result every week. They don't just want to be good, they want to dazzle everyone. "Wow! Wasn't that amazing? Amen! Now that's preaching!"

The truth is, the crowds gathered around the disciples were more impressed by *how* Jesus preached than by *what* he preached. "Did you hear that? He didn't even use footnotes or air quotes—that was all his own stuff! Amazing!"

What matters most about any sermon is how we respond to it. And we can respond to what Jesus has just told us in all kinds of different ways.

Jesus has just told us how we are to live in relation to God and each other; how we are to seek God's kingdom and not our own; how we are to form our kingdom hearts that desire to follow after Jesus and store up our treasure in heaven, not right here where it won't last.

How can we respond to all this? We have options.

We can *reject* it.

Lots of people in Jesus' time took this option—especially the spiritual leaders (scribes and Pharisees). They had too much to lose by obeying what Jesus was calling for—their prominence and prestige, their power and their very livelihood. They aren't the only ones. That still happens all around us.

Criticizing Jesus and especially his church is a growth industry these days—but you don't have to be someone like Richard Dawkins or Christopher Hitchens to reject Jesus. All you need to do is realize what Jesus is calling you to do is crazy, way too old-fashioned, or impossible and you have rejected Jesus's teaching. You can try to be cynical like some high-powered intellectual (even though you can't even spell "intellectual") and say all this Jesus stuff is for weaklings and hypocrites.

But the house built on rejection goes *splat!*

We can try to *neglect* it.

We know what Jesus says is right, but it's highly inconvenient. He wants us to be his disciples and go after the kingdom of God. We are more interested in being consumers and going shopping. So, we just try to ignore what Jesus is saying and hope that it will just go away.

But every once in a while, that gnawing feeling will come back, and it haunts us. We'll try to ignore it or drown it with some other creature comforts, but it won't go away.

Because the house built on neglect goes *splat*!

We might try to *understand* it.

We're big on that around here. We like to hear things, weighty things, eternal things, theological things. We love to see angels line dancing on a comma and the fireworks that explode when we understand the difference between infralapsarian and supralapsarian. We want to understand what Jesus says. We'll read sixty books about it and write three of our own.

But Jesus still says hearing the word is not enough. To hear something according to the New Testament means we get it, we understand it. But Jesus is saying it's not enough just to understand it.

Because the house built on understanding goes *splat*!

We could even *ponder* it.

Like that crowd surrounding Jesus, we could be amazed at how Jesus teaches or even with what he teaches. We can come to church and hear what Jesus says and be strangely warmed or blown right out of our boots, but it never gets beyond that.

"A Dream of Intentional Obedience"

Jesus tells us what he tells us not so our minds are blown, but so our lives are changed.

Because the house built on amazement goes *splat*!

So, what's left? Jesus doesn't even have to tell us straight out—these two little stories tell us what Jesus wants us to do. He's been setting us up for this since verse 13—he repeats one word nine times. It's such a little word that we might have missed it, if Jesus hadn't been pounding it into our collective skulls. It's the little word "*do.*" We don't have to be all that bright to get how Jesus wants us to respond to his teaching. Jesus is getting all "Nike® Swoosh" on us and is saying *just do it!* We can think of a thousand excuses right now to put it off until tomorrow. *Just do it!* There are so many other important things we need to get done. *Just do it!* Our lives are so full already. *Just do it*! We might look weird to others. *Just do it*! We might have to say goodbye to some cherished habits. *Just do it*! Our lives might change directions. *Just do it*! What more do we need to hear? *Just do it! Just do it!*

2

Preaching Poetic Biblical Texts

Poetry is high voltage language. Poets appeal to our emotions and desire to affect us at the deepest level of our souls. Poetry is also highly patterned and figurative literature. The depth of thought and emotion that poets pour into their work is designed to elicit a corresponding deep reaction in the reader/hearer. Poetry can be untidy and uncomfortable at times as it addresses the painful as well as the praiseworthy.

Biblical poetry in general, and the Psalms in particular, has long been part of the Christian spiritual tradition but more as prayers and songs in private and corporate worship. Preaching biblical poetry is somewhat demanding if the preacher is to emulate the levels of emotion inherent with the poetic texts themselves. This may seem too far out of reach for the emotionally-reserved preacher. The pure visceral emotion as well as no-holds-barred lamenting may seem out of place in the Christian pulpit. But in the same way that the rest of the Bible is God showing how he speaks to us, biblical poetry is where he shows us how we might speak to him. Biblical poetry is concentrated in the Psalms, of course, but is found in prophetic books as well as sprinkled throughout narrative, wisdom, apocalyptic, and epistolary genres.

Challenges in preaching poetic texts include the preacher's proclivity to make every sermon sound like it's expositing an Epistle instead of a poem and finding a way to communicate deep emotion in a way that engages the congregation and does not require the preacher to have an out-of-body experience. Poems should be preached in their entirety (with the possible exception of Psalm 119), since their resolution seldom comes before the end. Preaching psalms may be where we make judicious use of other poetry to adopt the mood of the text.

"Kiss the Risen Son!"

Psalm 2, ESV
Easter 2016

PRAYER FOR ILLUMINATION:

LORD, we are beside ourselves with Easter joy! We celebrate the resurrection of Jesus like it was a downpour after a long drought. His life brings us life and we're in a celebrating mood. All we have now and all we're going to have when you return are because of the victory of Easter morning. Point our praise and direct our devotion, O LORD. And may the words of my mouth and the meditations of all our hearts be pleasing in your sight, O LORD, our Rock and our Redeemer. Amen.

SERMON:

Good late morning and welcome to the Late Morning Show. I'm your host, David "Psalman." We're going to get started with one of our Top Ten Lists, so I hope you're ready.

These are the top ten political disasters. So,

NUMBER 10: The Crusades—who thought torture evangelism would prove to be so unpopular?

NUMBER 9: Napoleon's Invasion of Russia—a big idea by a little man.

NUMBER 8: The League of Nations—for all you World War I fanatics—it was a league that was both pointless and powerless, kind of like the CFL.

NUMBER 7: Nazi Book Burning in Berlin—So Herr Hitler, book burning just makes people more curious.

Number 6: Bombing Pearl Harbor—if the bear's asleep, don't poke it with a sharp stick.

Number 5: The Bay of Pigs fiasco—if you want to take over Cuba, just send a million tourists.

Number 4: The Green Party—the only successful green party is the one after the Roughriders win the Grey Cup.

Number 3: The plan to legalize marijuana in Canada—a big "high"-five, Ottawa!

Number 2: Donald Trump's Twitter account—it speaks for itself.

And the Number 1 Political Disaster: Kings Rebelling Against the Lord's Anointed—no, really!

You may question what all this has to do with Psalm 2.

Good question. Here's what: Psalm 2 is a celebration psalm with an attitude. It uses all the sarcasm and irony of a late-night talk show host to celebrate the unparalleled power of the Lord and his anointed Son. Psalm 2 is an Easter psalm even before there was Easter. This psalm struts. This psalm has swagger. This psalm has attitude. This psalm is a celebration.

And about now, we're ready for a celebration. We've been getting ready for this for weeks now. It's called the season of Lent. At Caronport Community Church, we've been looking at the psalms of communal lament all through Lent. We now know it's OK not to be OK. But now we're ready to celebrate; it's party time!

That's the Easter order—preparation and then party. That's backwards to everywhere else. I have cousins who live down in New Orleans. Down there they have a carnival (heavy on the carnal) called Mardi Gras. That's French for Fat Tuesday. It's the day before Lent begins. Down there they spend weeks partying their brains out because they know Lent is coming and they are going to have to behave. They say, "Party now, pay for it later." For them Lent is one long hangover.

But for us, it's preparation first and then party.

Psalm 2 was written for a party. It was written originally to celebrate the coronation, or the anointing of the King of Judah in Jerusalem. This would mark a national celebration as everyone would gather to welcome their new king. But even more than their earthly king, this psalm is a celebration of the heavenly King.

"Kiss the Risen Son!"

So how do you celebrate the reign of the heavenly King and his Anointed One? You celebrate by showing why this King is above all other kings. There's this huge ceremony where everyone pays homage to the King.

It's been a long time since we've seen a coronation (just ask Prince Charles). It was back in 1953. To crown the monarch in Britain, there needs to be all the right people and all the proper trappings—the right throne on top of the right stone in the right costume with the right crown, and it goes on and on. By the time it's done we're left wondering, "Who would ever dare serve another?"

So, the psalmist himself gets the party started in the first three verses of this psalm: "Why do the nations rage and the peoples plot in vain? The kings of the earth set themselves, and the rulers take counsel together, against the LORD and his Anointed, saying, 'Let us burst their bonds apart and cast away their cords from us.'"

So, if the Lord is Lord of lords and King of kings, why do the other nations even put up a fight? Why bother trying to rise up against him? Look at what you're doing. Resistance is futile! All your talk of rebellion is just hot air.

Historically, whenever a ruling king died and was succeeded by his heir, this time of transition was often exploited by those nations who had been conquered. They would figure, "Now's our chance to rebel. We'll rise up now while the new king is just a rookie and they are all preoccupied with other matters."

We can see these conquered kings sitting around a big conference table wracking their collective brains as to how they could rebel. There are all kinds of murmuring coming from the room. As a matter of fact, the word the psalmist uses for "plotting" means to murmur or even grumble. It's the same word used in Psalm 1 to describe how we meditate on God's Law.

So, the psalmist calls them out. "What are you guys smoking? Why even bother? You look ridiculous!" But these kings do not always see what we see—especially back in the days of Judah. Judah was never really a world power. So those kings around Judah would have a different perspective. They weren't looking at this new king through the eyes of the chosen people. They might be saying, "What is all this crowing about?" They see Judah like this mouthy little kid in the playground saying, "My Dad can whip your dad!" And this guy's dad is just five feet tall and weighs 120 pounds soaking wet.

So maybe we're writing checks with our mouths that the bank won't cash. I wonder what God himself says about all this. We find out in the next three verses: "He who sits in the heavens laughs; the Lord holds them in derision. Then he will speak to them in his wrath and terrify them with his fury, saying, 'As for me, I have set my King on Zion, my holy hill.'"

This is God's response to those who are plotting rebellion—he laughs at them. There are different kinds of laughing. There is "funny-haha," which is simply humorous—like why did the chicken cross the road? Then there's "funny-aha," or the laughter of discovery—like isn't that funny that when I put a fork in the toaster I get a shock? And then there's "funny-nana," or mocking laughter—like saying, "Is that your face or did your neck throw up?"

God's laughter is this third kind—the "Are you kidding me?" kind of laughing. The picture I get is of a 280-pound linebacker looking down on a 180-pound receiver whom he has just pounded into the turf and saying, "Wooo, how do you like me now, baby?"

This is God, enthroned in the heavens, the Creator and Sustainer of all things, looking down on these posturing little potentates, saying, "O come on—really? This is my King whom I set up in my city on my holy hill—and you have the nerve to want to rise up against him?" If these kings have any sense at all, they will be shaking in their royal boots.

But now it's time for the king himself to speak up: "I will tell of the decree: The LORD said to me, 'You are my Son; today I have begotten you. Ask of me, and I will make the nations your heritage, and the ends of the earth your possession. You shall break them with a rod of iron and dash them in pieces like a potter's vessel.'"

Back in Judah's day, their kings were considered to be sons of God—not gods themselves, like in the neighboring nations. Their king was to represent his Father and to rule righteously according to the Law.

Now here is where this psalm takes on a brand-new significance for us. It's hard for us to think of this psalm referring to the kings of Judah—at least with a straight face. Even later generations of the Jews had trouble with this. We see all this royal coronation talk in light of the ultimate Anointed One—the Messiah.

So did the New Testament writers. Psalm 2 is the most quoted psalm in all the New Testament. And Paul, when he is preaching the gospel to those in Pisidian Antioch in Acts 13 says, "And we bring you the good news that what God promised to the fathers, this he has fulfilled to us their children by raising Jesus, as also it is written in the second Psalm, 'You are my Son, today I have begotten you.'"

It's Jesus who is the one who fulfills this psalm. God calls him Son at his baptism, in the transfiguration, and at his resurrection. Paul writes to the

Romans about this Son "who was descended from David according to the flesh and was declared to be the Son of God in power according to the Spirit of holiness by his resurrection from the dead, Jesus Christ our Lord" (Rom 1:3b–4).

It is Jesus who has been given the nations as his heritage and the ends of the earth as his possession. He is the One who breaks them with a rod of iron and dashes them in pieces like a potter's vessel.

This sounds a bit violent for the prince of peace but simply refers to what often happened back in ancient times at a coronation. The surrounding nations were written on clay tablets, then the new king would take his royal scepter and smash these tablets as a sign of his sovereignty. Jesus is this sovereign one.

So now we have this trio of voices joined together—the psalmist, God himself, and the Anointed One—the Messiah. And what are they saying? They're saying you don't mess with the Messiah.

It's no use trying to fight him—he is the King and everything belongs to him. Or to parody the words of the late Jim Crocé: "You don't tug on Superman's cape. You don't spit into the wind. You don't pull the mask of that old Lone Ranger and you don't mess around with *him*!"

So, what remains? How can we respond? The psalmist is back speaking now, and he is telling us: "Now therefore, O kings, be wise; be warned, O rulers of the earth. Serve the LORD with fear and rejoice with trembling. Kiss the Son, lest he be angry, and you perish in the way, for his wrath is quickly kindled. Blessed are all who take refuge in him."

Here's what we can do when we come face to face with the true King. You rebellious ones—don't rise up, wise up! Serve him with reverent fear because the fear of the Lord is the beginning of wisdom. And come to him in repentance and submission and kiss him. This used to happen back in the day as well. Those under the sovereignty of the new king would come forward and bow reverently and kiss his feet.

There really is no other response that makes sense. Only in Jesus, the risen Son, there is salvation. Those who hide their lives in his will be truly blessed. He covers our sins with his perfect sacrifice and his resurrected life gives us new life. Today is a time to celebrate brand new life. And for those of us who have found this life, to those of us who have kissed the Son, he offers his gracious invitation to come and eat with him. This King calls us to share in his table. So, it is entirely appropriate to conclude our celebration by celebrating Communion together—in it we experience the power of his death and the promise of his resurrected life.

"A Wedding Fit for a King"

Psalm 45, ESV
December 8, 2013, Advent II

Series Title: "Psalms of the Savior"

PRAYER FOR ILLUMINATION

LORD we come before you this morning thoroughly amazed at your power and majesty and how one so mighty can be so loving—especially when we are so undeserving. We want to be more than amazed, we want to be moved to love like you do. So, may the words of my mouth and the meditations of all our hearts be pleasing in your sight, O LORD, our Rock and our Redeemer. Amen.

SERMON

[Video clip from the wedding scene of *Princess Bride*, including the "famous" "*Mawwiage* is why we are here today."]

Marriage *is* what brings us together today. Not the one on the screen, but the marriage of the true King, the Anointed One to his princess bride. Psalm 45 is a royal psalm, or we might call it a messianic psalm, but it's a royal psalm with a twist. It's a royal wedding song—a love song for the King's wedding day. There are other love songs in the Bible. The Song of Songs (or Solomon) is a love song. But Psalm 45 is a love song for the wedding day. Song of Songs sounds like it's for the honeymoon!

Back in the time of ancient Israel, a royal wedding would be a great celebration. It would take place with all kinds of fanfare as the bride made the very public move from her own house to the palace of the king. So, we

"A Wedding Fit for a King"

could imagine all this happening against the backdrop of the king's palace, of maybe even the temple in Jerusalem. Maybe you could imagine what it would be like to have the whole back of the stage look like the temple and have this whole spectacle happen before our eyes.

As we imagine what it might have looked like back then, we need to remember what we learned last week. Even though these psalms were written originally to relate to the life of Israel's king, they began to realize none of their kings, even King David, could measure up to the picture painted in these royal psalms. So they began to see them through two different lenses—one referring to their own king and the other to the real anointed One, the coming Messiah.

That's the kind of lenses I'm wearing this morning, and maybe some of the rest of you are too. They're called bifocals. Not the kind with the line through them, but the progressive ones. As I look out these lenses, I can see clearly close up and clearly far away just by looking through a different part of the same lens. And that's how we read these royal psalms. We know this wedding song refers to Israel's king but also to our King—Jesus.

Today we are invited to a royal wedding. There are some things we might expect when we are invited to a wedding. We might expect it to be all about the bride and groom, and we can expect the wedding to be a combination of celebration and commitment (since both have to make vows during the ceremony). It's an exciting thing to be invited to a royal wedding—we should be thrilled to be here. The psalmist is. Just listen to him: "My heart overflows with a pleasing theme; I address my verses to the king; my tongue is like the pen of a ready scribe" (Ps 45:1). He can't wait to blurt out all that he sees unfolding before him.

Most attention on wedding days today is focused on the bride, but here we're at the wedding of the king and so he's the one on center stage. He's the one being celebrated, and I mean celebrated. Listen to how the psalmist describes how he looks: "You are the most handsome of the sons of men; grace is poured upon your lips; therefore God has blessed you forever . . . your robes are all fragrant with myrrh and aloes and cassia. From ivory palaces stringed instruments make you glad; daughters of kings are among your ladies of honor; at your right hand stands the queen in gold of Ophir" (Ps 45:2, 8, 9). All that is pretty impressive—stuff you might expect when the king is getting married. He's quite the sight. We almost need sunglasses he's so bright and dazzling.

But the psalmist doesn't stop there. Not only does he describe what the king's like on the outside, next he tells us what he's like on the inside: "Your throne, O God, is forever and ever. The scepter of your kingdom is a scepter of uprightness; you have loved righteousness and hated wickedness; therefore God, your God has anointed you with the oil of gladness beyond your companions." When someone is addressing their king on his wedding day, you might expect him to go "a bit over the top"—maybe you can remember a few years back to the wedding of Will and Kate. Talk about over the top! But did you notice that the psalmist is referring to the king when he says, "Your throne, O God, is forever and ever."? That's more than over the top. Remember that in Israel, their kings were not considered to be divine, they were adopted sons of Yahweh and not gods in their own right.

This only makes sense when we look at this psalm through the other part of our bifocals. The New Testament writers understood this could only refer to Jesus when all was said and done. The writer to the Hebrews is referring to Jesus when he quotes these verses from Psalm 45: "But of the Son he says, 'Your throne, O God, is forever and ever, the scepter of uprightness is the scepter of your kingdom. You have loved righteousness and hated wickedness; therefore God, your God, has anointed you with the oil of gladness beyond your companions.'"

We are not only called to celebrate the King, we hear that he has vows to make, promises to keep. The psalmist calls on the king in verses 3–5: "Gird your sword on your thigh, O mighty one, in your splendor and majesty! In your majesty ride out victoriously for the cause of truth and meekness and righteousness; let your right hand teach you awesome deeds! Your arrows are sharp in the heart of the king's enemies; the peoples fall under you." The king is called to vow that he will be kingly and act righteously and conquer his enemies victoriously. He's not to use his power to feather his own nest but to care for those he is leading.

Along with these vows come promises because promises are a big part of a wedding ceremony. So, if the king does indeed act kingly, God will keep the promises he makes to him: "In place of your fathers shall be your sons; you will make them princes in all the earth. I will cause your name to be remembered in all generations; therefore, nations will praise you forever and ever" (vv. 16–17).

So far, all our eyes have been on the king, and that's only right since he's the royal one. But there is someone else who is part of this day. After all, it takes two to do the wedding tango. The psalmist also leads us to celebrate the princess bride. "All glorious is the princess in her chamber, with robes interwoven with gold. In many-colored robes she is led to the king, with her virgin companions following behind her. With joy and gladness, they are led along as they enter the palace of the king" (vv. 13–15). This is the part in modern weddings when the congregation stands and the bridal party starts their processional down the aisle. Everyone is gasping and weeping. The whole thing is a spectacle. The princess doesn't just have to come down an aisle, but she has to proceed to the king's palace in rainbow robes with the golden fabric glistening in the sun. All her bridesmaids follow after her as they make their way to the palace.

When she arrives, she too must make some vows herself: "Hear O daughter, and consider, and incline your ear: forget your people and your father's house . . . Since he is your Lord, bow to him" (vv. 10–11). This might sound a bit archaic to our ears. I sense a little squirming among the brides and the brides-to-be in the room. But this was spoken first to the brides of the kings of Israel who were often from foreign countries. Queens who didn't forget their homelands brought havoc and idol worship to Israel—the many wives of Solomon and Queen Jezebel are cases in point.

She is also to bow to him because even though she is the queen, she also is to serve the king. The king is everyone's king.

Along with her vows, she too will receive promises. These are found in verses 11 and 12. If she is faithful to her vows, the psalmist tells her, "the king will desire your beauty" (v. 11). And, secondly, if she becomes queen, she will be treated as a queen: "The people of Tyre will seek your favor with gifts, the richest of the people" (v. 12).

It's probably about now that something weird starts to happen to us. Instead of looking back into the times of Israel's kings, we are overwhelmed by the sense that we're not looking at the bride of some ancient king. We are looking at the bride of the Messiah, the bride of Christ, and that is us, the church. And then all the vows and the promises start to make sense.

If we are to be the bride of Christ, we're asked to forget our past. It doesn't matter where we've come from, Jesus gathers us as his bride. Our past is just that—past tense. Jesus died for us while we were still sinners, still rebelling against him. That past is washed away, and he calls us not to worry about where we came from. That's all been taken care of.

And if we're the bride of Christ, we're to serve him. He's our Lord. We're called to love and obey him. As Paul says, "Wives, submit to your own husbands, as to the Lord. For the husband is the head of the wife even as Christ is the head of the church, his body, and is himself its Savior" (Eph 5:22–23).

The most amazing part of this wedding is the promise part. We are promised as the bride of Christ that we will always be loved by the King. Like Paul mentions, "Husbands, love your wives, as Christ loved the church and gave himself up for her, that he might sanctify her, having cleansed her by the washing of water with the word, so that he might present the church to himself in splendor, without spot or wrinkle or any such thing, that she might be holy and without blemish" (Eph 5:25–27).

Part of that love is his promise to us that, on one special day, he will come for us and we will be his holy bride. All the work, trouble, stress, and strain will seem to vanish. I have performed many weddings over the years. Many times, at the wedding rehearsal, I've noticed how the bride-to-be is stressed and worn out. But something miraculous always happens overnight—on the wedding day she's not bothered, she's beautiful. She's not stressed, she's stunning!

Christ can hardly wait for that day. He is dwelling in the heavenly throne room and is saying with anticipation, "Surely I am coming soon!" That great day when we appear before him in complete purity, without spot or blemish. Every groom in the crowd can remember that same experience that happened to me over thirty one years ago to me. When the back doors of the church open and there is your beautiful bride—radiant in a cloud of white, hanging on to her father's arm, otherwise the cloud of white lace would whisk her straight into heaven.

Are you still wondering why we make such a big deal about weddings? Why weddings cost so much for just one day? Or why we should pay attention to the wedding of an Israelite king or our wedding as the bride of Christ? It's because weddings are never just about the wedding day. They all point to the future. The wedding is just the beginning of what lies ahead. So, we are called to forget what is in our past, to serve him in the present, knowing that no matter what happens, he loves us and is coming back for us. We know that day is coming—and it might be sooner than we think. So, with great joy we can join our voices and cry out together, "Amen, come Lord Jesus!"

"When We Feel Depressed"

Psalms 42–43, ESV
March 4, 2018

Series Title: "The Kiss of Jesus: Suffering and the Christian Life"

PRAYER FOR ILLUMINATION

LORD, we know our lives are fragile—they seem to dangle from a string. At times even that string seems frayed and at risk of breaking. It's during these times that we remember how much we depend on you. So, this morning we come to you as your needy children, seeking to hear from you about those times when we don't seem to hear from you. Speak so we can hear your voice. And may the words of my mouth and meditations of all our hearts be pleasing in your sight, O LORD, our Rock and our Redeemer. Amen.

SERMON

The statistics are alarming. As Canadians we are suffering from an epidemic of depression. That can range from bouts of sadness, to clinical depression, to seasonal affective disorder (SAD) that hits many this time of year, to experiencing the dark night of the soul as we struggle with the sense that God has abandoned us. About one in ten Canadians will suffer from serious clinical depression at some point in life, and the incidence of depression among the Millennial and Gen Z generations is skyrocketing. We have many things that we share in common—but one of them is that *all* of us know what it is like to experience bouts of sadness or depression. Some are suggesting Canada is heading into the second Great Depression. If the first

Depression was the Dirty Thirties, then we are living in the Mean Teens, and this time it could be even worse psychologically, if not economically.

That, in itself, is a bit depressing, isn't it?

Here's a question for you: What do you do when you are feeling sad or depressed, when your whole body seems to slow down, and any effort seems too much, when you feel like garbage, hopeless, and all by yourself? I had a former professor who said he often felt so low that he would have to step on a brick to spank a duck. What do you do when there's not a brick in sight?

You sing, right? Maybe not. But some do. Some of the most powerful music comes out of these times of intense suffering: the blues, the great spirituals, spawned out of the cesspool of slavery.

So, what can we do when we're feeling sad, alone, and depressed? We can sing—even when we don't feel like singing, we can sing—not happy, sappy, clappy songs, but songs that lift our pain to the God who seems to have gone AWOL, at least for the moment.

We can sing this song of the sons of Korah; these guys know how to lament—I call them the Blues Brothers. That's what the Psalms do. God speaks *to* us in the Bible—but in the Psalms, God speaks *for* us.

This morning the Blues Brothers want to teach us how to sing—how to sing with feeling. [Sing in deep, mournful tones]:

"Nobody knows the trouble I've seen—nobody knows but Jesus."

These two psalms break down into three stanzas and each of them has the same chorus: "Why are you cast down. O my soul, and why are you in turmoil within me? Hope in God; for I shall again praise him, my salvation and my God" (see Ps 42:5, 11; Ps 43:5).

This is a sermon, not a counselling session, and the sons of Korah are not sons of a counsellor, nor am I, but here we can find real help when we feel the most helpless.

The psalm begins where most of us begin—with our complaint. We usually say it this way: "Why me? Why this? Why now?"

This is how the psalmist puts it: "As a deer pants for flowing streams, so pants my soul for you, O God. My soul thirsts for God, for the living God. When shall I come and appear before God?" (Ps 42:1–2).

You can feel the longing in these words—there is a dryness and a desperation that flies right off the page. Maybe you've felt this dryness yourself—like life has just shriveled up, like you're hollow, on empty, and there's nothing left in the tank except to wish for something better. I almost get dry mouth just speaking these words.

These are the desperate cries of someone who wants to reach out and feel refreshed by God, but there is nothing but hot, dry desert. The psalmist looks behind himself, and all he sees for miles around is sand under the scorching of an angry sun.

What he remembers is constant weeping and the taunts of those around who seem to take perverse joy in the fact he is all alone and God is nowhere in sight.

If that's not bad enough, he remembers the good old days when he used to sense God's presence as he led God's people in worship as they entered the temple courts during the religious festivals. The sons of Korah were temple musicians. They remembered the times when they were up leading worship; they could almost reach out and touch God in the praises of his people.

But that was then . . . and this is now. [Sing again]:

"Nobody knows the trouble I've seen, nobody knows but Jesus."

And so, the psalmist stops looking back and starts looking around. The present is the same mixed bag as the past. He started by longing for water to quench his thirst for God, and now he feels completely drowned by waves that are seeking to destroy him. For him, it literally never rains, but it pours.

He speaks of "deep calls to deep." Most of us think this might be a good thing—it sounds so . . . deep. But the depths were those chaotic waters God had to tame back when he created the world. These are waves calling to each other to swamp your canoe way out in the middle of Northumberland Strait so that you never see another day.

There are things we know in our heads, but they never make their way down to our hearts.

We know in our heads that verse 8 is true: "By day the LORD commands his steadfast love, and at night his song is with me, a prayer to the God of my life."

But the reality seems far removed. We wonder, "'Where is that steadfast love and that song and those prayers? All I see around me are smug jerks who love rubbing my nose in my suffering.' They are constantly badgering me, 'So where is this God of yours? If you are so holy, why are you so miserable?'"

It's easy enough to get trapped into thinking that something has gone terribly wrong here. Either it's God's fault and he hasn't lived up to his part of the bargain, having taken a vacation to leave me twisting in the wind, or it's my own fault and there is something wrong with my faith, or I wouldn't be feeling this way. This can be a losing battle, and we can end up spiraling downward because we are looking for the answer in the wrong direction.

This only begins to turn around for the psalmist in the third verse— what we know as Psalm 43. There is nothing magical or immediate here— the psalms weren't written in Hollywood. No pixie dust, cheesy epiphany, or tear-jerking music. We have to look closely even to see it.

Looking back hasn't helped, nor has looking around. Nothing changes until we look up. Here is where the psalmist's perspective shifts from himself to God and he starts to plead his case directly to him.

"Vindicate me, O God, and defend my cause against an ungodly people, from the deceitful and unjust man, deliver me!" and "Send out your light and your truth; let them lead me; let them bring me to your holy hill and to your dwelling!" (Ps 43:1–3).

There is no thunderbolt from heaven. The suffering doesn't suddenly disappear. The psalmist still is saying he feels rejected by God and is still surrounded by all these jeering enemies. So, what has changed? Nothing, in one sense, but in another sense, everything.

Until now, all is wrapped in darkness and suffering, but now there is hope of a light. He doesn't even see it now, but he knows it's coming. Now he can see himself back with God's people, leading them in worship— somehow in the meantime he's learned to play a new instrument, so soon he'll be leading with his lungs and the lyre! And it's all because God's light and his truth has led him back to where he belongs—to worship.

And the psalmist concludes with the chorus—again. But this time, we get it. We might have been singing it without even understanding it, but now it comes out of the shadows and into the light. "Why are you cast down, O my soul, and why are you in turmoil within me? hope in God; for I shall again praise him, my salvation and my God" (Ps 43:5).

The emphasis is no longer on [singing]: "Nobody knows the trouble I've seen," but it moves to [singing]: "Nobody knows but Jesus!"

We have moved from the turmoil within our souls to our hope in God. We have moved from hopeless to helpless to hopeful. And that has happened by taking the focus off ourselves and putting it on God. That means trusting God enough to wait for him to do his good work in his time.

"When We Feel Depressed"

The truth of the matter is we will never understand our suffering by looking back and all around trying to figure out where it came from. It's often way too involved and mysterious for that. That's usually above our pay grade. We bear with suffering in all its forms not by looking back or around, but by looking to where it leads (or better, to whom it leads).

That may be quite a bit to take in all from one song. But the thing about good songs is they are never meant to be sung just once. The better the song, the more it needs to be sung. Some songs are so bad you only need to sing them once—this is not one of those.

So, for those of you who are bit more left-brained and would like it better in point form, let me indulge you.

What do we do when we're depressed?

We name the elephant. There is no use denying what God and everyone else knows. If we are sad or depressed, that doesn't mean we want to stay there, so we might as well admit it. All of us will suffer this way at some time and to some extent. We are all weak and we all struggle. We are all egotists. Some of us are better at hiding it than others. It ain't pretty, but it's real.

We stay connected. Part of sadness and depression is the sense we are all alone. To withdraw from everyone else just makes it worse. What is true for the Blues Brothers is true for us—we are never happier than when we are with God's people, singing and worshipping and eating, caring and eating, and helping and eating together. So, we can sing together, "Hope in God!"

Keep on hoping. Our focus needs to be on God and his goodness even while things are still bad—even when we feel abandoned and even while our enemies keep giving us a hard time. Hoping on God means to wait for God—to trust his tomorrow more than obsess over today. This is how our salvation comes to us in this sinful world. The injustice of today is made right tomorrow; the tears of today are wiped away tomorrow; the sorrow of Good Friday is swallowed up in the joy of Easter Sunday. And that's the way it is for those of us who are living somewhere in between the two. We have every reason to sing together, [singing], "Somebody knows the troubles we've seen—and his name is Jesus!"

"When We Feel Surrounded"

Psalm 12, ESV
February 21, 2016, Lent II

Series Title: "Cries of Desperate Hope"

PRAYER FOR ILLUMINATION

LORD, we know you are our Rock and Refuge when we feel like our worlds are falling apart. We cling to your comforting presence and faithful word when everything else gives way. We know we are prone to exaggerate our difficulties, but you take our cries seriously, which is why we bring them to you. So, may the words of my mouth and the meditations of all our hearts be pleasing in your sight, O LORD, our Rock and our Redeemer. Amen.

SERMON

To be honest I'm a bit afraid we all might need neck braces this morning as we move from the high energy of Youth Quake (high energy youth conference hosted on campus) last week to a sermon series on communal laments in the Psalms this week. It's like difference between driving from Disneyland to Death Valley. That's enough to give us a serious case of whiplash.

But I think it's worth the risk—and here's why. We would like to live all of life on top of the mountain, but we know a good portion of life is spent in the valley. That's just the way it is. We might try to deny it or downplay it, but deep in our hearts we know it's there. And guess what, so does God. So what God has done is give us inspired examples of how we can approach him in prayer no matter how we might be feeling at the time. There is a psalm for every mood. Writer Anne Lamott says there are really only three basic prayers: help, thanks, and wow. Old Testament scholar Walter Brueggemann puts it another way. He says there are psalms of orientation for when life is the way it should be, and there are psalms of disorientation when everything seems to have fallen apart and we're in the pit or the depths or Sheol. Then there are psalms of re-orientation when God has delivered us out of the pit and we want to thank him. Life tends to be a rhythm of being in and out of the pit.

A lament is prayer language for us when we're in the pit. It's not a hopeless whining about what will never change. It is a cry of desperate hope to the only One who can deliver us out of the pit. We're doing this not just because it is the season of Lent or we just want to wallow in self-pity. Laments are actually very hopeful and honest worship—we don't do "lament" very well in the church. Jesus died with two laments on his lips: "My God, my God, why have you forsaken me?" from Psalm 22 and "into your hands do I commit my spirit" taken from Psalm 31—both lament psalms.

There are not many good examples of lament in the church, so today we need to look outside for some help. In some ways, rap music is a kind of lament. But probably the best example would be one of those hurting songs that you can only get in Country and Western music. Probably the saddest of them all is the classic by Hank Williams, "Your Cheatin' Heart."

Maybe you're like me and wonder what it would sound like if a country singer wrote Psalm 12. [Sung with accompanying cowboy hat and guitar with a nasal twang]:

> Their cheatin' lips are everywhere
> They lie and brag and curse and swear
> They pick on us continually
> Their cheatin' lips are killing me.
>
> Their flattering lips cause us to pray
> "Lord, chop their lips right off today!"
> They make us feel like we are dirt
> Their flattering lips really hurt.
>
> But God will stand and speak his Word
> Then we won't care what we have heard
> Then we will change the way we feel
> Their cheatin' lips are no big deal.

So how do we pray when we feel surrounded?

We start, like the psalmist, with a cry: "Save, O LORD."

This is not a throwaway phrase. It points us to the whole power of prayer. This is what separates a lament from just plain whining. We take our troubles to God—we don't just grumble to ourselves or to anyone else who might listen. Turning inside ourselves can lead to depression as we sink further in and our world just keeps getting darker. Turning outside and venting on others just makes us grouchy and whiny and eventually lonely as we drive away even those who want to help. Our only true option is to look upward.

Prayer is the cry of the needy heart. Part of the trouble we face in prayer is few of us really know what it's like to be needy. True, we all have our moments when it seems like life is spiraling out of control. But most of the time we are afflicted with affluence and delusions of our own ability to fix what only God can fix. So, it's hard for us to get into the mindset of true desperation. But a lament is the recognition of our desperation and is a hopeful cry to God to save us.

Usually praise psalms start with praise to God and then give the reason for that praise. Laments usually begin with this cry to God and then give the reason for that cry—a complaint. Here's the psalmist's reason for his complaint: "for the godly one is gone; for the faithful have vanished from among the children of man. Everyone utters lies to his neighbor; with flattering lips and a double heart they speak" (Psalm 12:1b–2).

Here's how we pray when we feel surrounded by liars. You'll notice the strong language here. There are no godly or faithful ones left and everyone is a liar. Poets don't speak like scientists. Poets exaggerate, and they do it on purpose—so we get what they are trying to say. Scientists communicate with precision—poets communicate with passion. Scientists would say 75 percent of society is prone to dishonesty in their speech when it is convenient. Poets say everyone is a liar—they're all smooth-talking, manipulative liars.

But we get the point. We get a sense of the burden here. God's people are feeling alone and isolated. Their trust in others is shattered because it looks like no one tells the truth. Who can they believe? They feel alone. It's not hard to see how this can be similar to the situation we face today. Liars are everywhere: we have just come through a federal election; we are in the midst of a provincial election and the presidential primaries in the US; and it is income tax time. Maybe we feel like people have lied to us—maybe it's our parents, or teachers, or boss or the church. We wonder if anyone can be trusted. Everyone has their own spin on their truth. That can make us feel like we're all alone—a bit like Elijah when he complained to God that he was the only righteous one left in Israel. It wasn't true, but it felt like it.

The psalmist uses picture language here to express his passion. He says everyone is using flattering lips, which is literally "smooth" lips. You've heard of smooth-talkers before. That's what flattery is. It's lying designed to get something from someone else. When someone comes up to you and showers you with praise, what is your first impulse? You think they're up to something, right? When someone comes up to me after a service and says, "That's the best sermon I've ever heard," what is the first thing that goes through my head? It's, "I probably should preach louder because obviously this person is deaf, or they want something from me."

Not only do they have smooth lips, they have a double heart—literally, "a heart and a heart." It means they can't be trusted. They will speak out of one heart one day and their other heart the next—they have a heart for each of their faces.

These feel like drastic times, and so that calls for drastic measures. When we feel surrounded, not only do we call out to God and tell him our troubles, we usually want to help him by telling him how we want him to answer our prayer. Here's the solution of verse 3: "May the Lord cut off all flattering lips, the tongue that makes great boasts, those who say, "With our tongue we will prevail, our lips are with us; who is master over us?"

Here, God, is how you show these arrogant big talkers—they make such massive claims with those lips, maybe those lips should be cut right off, and then how could they mouth off?

This might strike us as a bit over the top—and it should. Is the real solution a massive "lip-ectomy"? But remember we're looking at poetry here—and poetry is passionate, not precise. Maybe we even feel a bit guilty when we get this carried away.

This is something we find within the psalms—we call them imprecatory psalms when we wish bad fortune on our enemies. Is this legitimate for those of us who have been called by Jesus to love our enemies? First, note that this is addressed to God and for his honor, not ours. And second, we aren't saying we are going to go out and cut people's lips off—we are calling on God to do it because we see these "lippy" people are not honoring God. They think they have no master. We're saying to God—"You show them they have a master and make the punishment fit the crime." There is a huge difference between revenge (which is us getting even) and vengeance (which is God doing the judging).

This still makes us nervous, but at least it's honest and it doesn't take matters into our own hands.

And as usually is the case, God doesn't need our help. He has an answer of his own: "'Because the poor are plundered, because the needy groan, I will now arise,' says the LORD; 'I will place him in the safety [literally, "I will give him the salvation"] for which he longs [literally, "that he pants for"]'" (v. 5).

Here, God responds to our lament, says he has seen our distress, and he will bring the salvation we are panting for. That's his answer—his word, a promise. He has seen our distress and he will send us deliverance. He doesn't come with a pair of big lip clippers. He doesn't send a massive lightning bolt to zap the bad guys. He utters a promise to the good guys. And that's it—nothing more. Is that really enough? How can we trust God's word when everyone else has lied to us? How can we tell the difference?

Then it dawns on us, "The words of the LORD are pure words, like silver refined in a furnace on the ground, purified seven times." God's word is like no other. It isn't sneaky, it isn't manipulative, it isn't self-serving. It is pure. Really pure—like the smelting process for silver. This is not just any smelting process, but this silver is put through the fire not once or twice but seven times. It is completely pure.

Back when our kids were smaller, and we would have a marshmallow roast, one of our children, who will remain nameless, had her own way of roasting a marshmallow. She would set it on fire until it was black and then eat that part and then put it back in the fire again and turn it black again. She would do this until the whole thing was gone. In the end the marshmallow was not partly carbon but completely carbon—100 percent carbon. Just like God's word is 100 percent pure.

So, now that God has weighed into our situation, how do we respond? Look at verses 7 and 8: "You, O LORD, will keep them; you will guard us from this generation forever. On every side the wicked prowl as vileness is exalted among the children of man."

Do you notice something? There has been a change but not in everything. The situation hasn't really changed yet. The wicked are still prowling around like lions and vileness is everywhere. But something has changed. It's us. What happened?

"When We Feel Surrounded"

God has spoken, and his word is pure. Everyone around us lies all the time and we can't trust anyone. God has spoken, and his word is pure. People don't like us and wish we would crash and burn. God has spoken, and his word is pure. It looks like we will never accomplish our mission, and people don't want to hear what we have to say. God has spoken, and his word is pure. It feels like we're surrounded and we're all alone. God has spoken, and his word is pure.

What do we do when we feel like we are surrounded and the faithful have vanished from the children of man? When we're all alone and we're at the end of our rope? We hold fast to one thing: God has spoken, and his word is pure. And that is enough.

"When We are Betrayed by a Friend"

Psalm 55, ESV
March 11, 2018

Series Title: "The Kiss of Jesus: Suffering and the Christian Life"

PRAYER FOR ILLUMINATION

LORD we praise you for your faithfulness to us when we all have felt what it's like to be betrayed in some way. This urge to think of ourselves rather than others is in all of us. We've felt its sting and we have stung others. Show us how we can be wronged without being wrong in return. Show us your way, O LORD. And may the words of my mouth and the meditations of all our hearts be pleasing in your sight, O LORD, our Rock and our Redeemer. Amen.

SERMON

Their pictures are all up there mounted on the wall in the Traitor's Hall of Shame: Brutus against Julius Caesar, Benedict Arnold in the Revolutionary War, Vidkun Quisling in World War II, and of course, Judas Iscariot. All these guys are despised because they represent what is ugly in all of us— turning on our closest friends and stabbing them in the back (in Brutus' case, literally) just for our own gain. All of us have this sense of special loathing for betrayers and traitors because all of us, at some point and to some degree, have felt what it's like to be betrayed. Maybe it was by a good friend, a boyfriend or girlfriend, a business partner, a colleague, a family member, or a spouse. We've all felt the icy kiss of betrayal.

"When We are Betrayed by a Friend"

What hurts the most about being betrayed is it never comes from our enemies—it always comes from someone within kissing distance. (Just ask Jesus.)

The whole experience of being betrayed disorients us because we never see it coming. We're all over the place, emotionally confused, angry, surprised, angry, in denial, angry. We're not sure how to respond—but usually some form of payback comes to mind rather quickly.

That leaves us with the burning question: How do we respond when we have been betrayed by someone close to us?

King David knows all about this. He even writes a song about it—we just read the lyrics. When you are king, you get used to people gunning for your job. Lots of David's songs deal with his enemies—usually he doesn't mention them by name, and that's OK because that allows us to fill in the blanks with our own enemies. These songs are full of raw, sometimes shocking emotions. Whether we like to admit it or not, David's emotions carry our own feelings up to God and we are able to let it all hang out in his presence.

We can see David is a bit messed up here—he can't believe he's been betrayed by a close friend—it even takes until verse 12 before he's able to admit it. This psalm goes all over the place—good luck trying to squeeze it into a logical outline. Outlining this psalm is a bit like dry shaving a dragon. Here's a guy struggling with betrayal.

How does he respond? And even more, how can we respond?

This is a lament, so David starts by lamenting. So, David would suggest we start by lodging our complaint. "Give ear to my prayer, O God, and hide not yourself from my plea for mercy! Attend to me and answer me; I am restless in my complaint and I moan, because of the oppression of the wicked. For they drop trouble upon me, and in anger they bear a grudge against me."

I'm not sure we always feel comfortable speaking to God this way. It's like busting through the curtain into the holy of holies, grabbing God by the collar, and demanding that he listen up. Most of us don't have that kind of *chutzpah*. But we do complain, don't we? We usually put it this way: Why me? Why this? Why now? Have those words ever gone through your mind or spewed from your lips to God?

We often feel guilty for telling God the truth. This is how we feel. Do we think he doesn't know? Do you think he'll say, "Thanks for bringing this up Blayne, I guess I just hadn't noticed."

The big issue here isn't *what* we say—it's *who* we say it to. We start by taking this to God—not by retaliating without even giving it a second thought. And usually our retaliation escalates out of control. Here's what often happens: we get betrayed and we say, "He stabbed me in the back and so I'm going to get a missile launcher and shoot him right in the face!" If revenge is our immediate response, we have lost the battle already. We need to follow David here and bring it to the Lord.

Obviously, David has more to say, and so do we when we have been betrayed. That means we go from lodging our complaint to acknowledging our pain. "My heart is in anguish within me; the terrors of death have fallen upon me. Fear and trembling come upon me, and horror overwhelms me."

Again, this language seems a bit over the top to most of us. David is sounding a bit like a drama king here. Even if this isn't the language we would use—because we aren't actual kings and people aren't out to actually kill us (usually)—we can at least identify with the depth of pain here.

When we have been betrayed by someone close to us, it feels like our world has collapsed in on us. We feel like we're going to suffocate. We depended on this person and they hurt us, really hurt us. We just need to tell the truth about that. Our complaint tells God that something is wrong—now we're telling him how that makes us feel. There's nothing wrong with that—actually it's the healthy thing to do. Bottling it up inside will just lead to an explosion later on. Then everyone will be wondering, "Where did that come from?"

Now after telling God how we're feeling about it, we can go on to catalogue our options. What are we going to do? How are we going to handle this betrayal?

David's first option is to run away. "And I say, 'Oh, that I had wings like a dove! I would fly away and be at rest; yes, I would wander far away; I would lodge in the wilderness; I would hurry to find a shelter from the raging wind and tempest'" (Ps 55:6–8).

Maybe we might be tempted to run away just to get away from the horrors of betrayal. The problem here is that doesn't deal with the problem. When you come back, even if you come back, the situation is the same—nothing has changed. The avoidance option is tempting but ultimately unfulfilling.

David moves on to vengeance. "Destroy, O Lord, divide their tongues; for I see violence and strife in the city. Day and night, they go around on its walls, and iniquity and trouble are within it; ruin is in its midst; oppression and fraud do not depart from its marketplace" (Ps 55:9–11).

We need to understand the difference between vengeance and revenge. Revenge is when we retaliate because we have been wronged and we want to get even. Vengeance is when we want justice rather than to get even. There have been wrongs committed and they need to be addressed. Revenge is something we take into our own hands. Vengeance is something we leave in God's hands. We remember God saying, "'Vengeance is mine, I will repay,' says the Lord" (Deut 32:35).

These enemies have been wreaking havoc on the city. They are violent, oppressive, and evil. They are holding the whole city hostage to their evil deeds and that needs to be addressed. This is David's plea to God. David isn't looking for personal revenge, he's looking to God for divine vengeance.

It's here that he finally admits his greatest enemy was once actually his friend. He actually interrupts himself and goes off on this bunny trail about how much this guy was his BFF. There is this slow motion flashback, and there are these two younger guys racing in their chariots, going to the Hebron 7-Eleven for a Slurpee run. Then they're sitting together in worship, laughing at the priest because he spit a lot when he preached. Have you ever had one of those episodes? It just makes it worse when you think of all the great times you had with this backstabber, doesn't it?

Then David's mind goes back to where he left off—seeking vengeance for all this injustice done. He asks God that death might sneak up on them—that they might slide down into Sheol—the place of the dead—while they were still alive.

David is still pretty upset here. He wants this guy gone. He's not going to do it himself—and we all know David is capable of doing something like this. And it's not just a matter of David hiring God as a heavenly hitman to do the dirty work for him. But wrongs have been done—in his words, "for evil is in their dwelling place and in their heart" (Ps 55:15b).

To this point, everything seems a bit negative, does it not? He's pouring out his wounded heart to God in this song, and all this hurt and anger is spilling out.

It makes me wonder what if David didn't write this song, but what if Christian recording artist Michael W. Smith did? What would it sound like? [Move behind the keyboard and simulate the introspective feel of the song.]

Pulling out the knife you've planted
Right between my vertebrae
Don't try to make those dumb excuses
'Cause I can't believe a single word you say.
But I'll watch you close as always
To see a betrayer at work
'Cause in my heart in big and small ways
You will always be a stupid jerk.

And friends aren't friends forever
If they stab you in the back
And a friend should not be nasty
Or give you all that flak.
It's not hard to let you go
'Cause you're headed for Sheol
For a lifetime of betraying your friends.

It's a good thing David doesn't leave it there. There is another option: trust. "But I call to God, and the LORD will save me" (v. 16). David trusts that God will hear his voice and deliver him. When his world is crumbling in on him, David can choose to trust in the God who hears and answers our pleas for help. The same holds true of us as well.

David is still very upset and so he heads back into another flashback. He still can't get over this betrayal. This friend has betrayed the covenant, the bond between them. His words are smooth and deceptive: smooth as butter, softer than oil, but meant to destroy. All this is still raw for David, as it is often with us. We have a hard time letting go.

We get right up to the last two verses of the psalm before we know what David is going to do. He's going to cast this burden on the Lord, he's going to trust in God and leave it all in his hands.

It's been a long journey and we've come to the end. David is going to trust God with this even though he still thinks this betrayer should die for all his sins. Is this the best we can hope for? Maybe. Maybe not.

As followers of Jesus, we can remember Jesus calling us to forgive those who have sinned against us. He calls us to love our enemies. Maybe there is something more. It's not just a matter of W.W.D.D.? (What Would David Do?). What is it that pleases Jesus?

We know Jesus felt the sting of betrayal. His cheek felt the icy wound of the kiss of Judas. He's been there. He knows how it feels. And he willingly

"When We are Betrayed by a Friend"

died for everyone who would betray a friend—and that's all of us. We can trust Jesus, even when we can't trust anyone else.

As followers of Jesus, our main concern, as it turns out, is not with the kiss of Judas—the suffering of betrayal from a friend. Our main concern is the kiss of Jesus—where Jesus promises to be with us in this kind of suffering as in all kinds of suffering. The kiss of Jesus is the promise that even the deepest suffering can be redeemed at the cross. The kiss of Jesus means we can forgive because we have been forgiven. We can love because we have been loved. So, the next time we are stabbed in the back or kicked to the curb by a friend, we have someone to turn to: the One who has turned his other cheek, who forgives us for the times we have betrayed him, the One whose friendship never fails and whose kiss brings us life.

"A Whole New Kind of Hero"

Isaiah 42:1–9, ESV
June 14, 2015

Series Title: "The Fifth Gospel: Isaiah's Message for Us"

PRAYER FOR ILLUMINATION

LORD, we thank you for how you have been our Leader and our Lord—leading us where we need to go and showing us how to lead in the process. Forgive us for the times when we have misunderstood what it means to lead—when we have been missing either grace or truth. And may the words of my mouth and meditations of all our hearts be pleasing in your sight, O LORD, our Rock and our Redeemer. Amen.

SERMON

If you have a bulletin, I'd invite you to pull out the insert from the Global Leadership Summit we're hosting this fall. It says something that maybe you don't believe. In all capital letters it says, "YOU ARE A LEADER." Maybe you don't buy that. It could be you think you are not a leader. The truth is—you are. Everyone is a leader. Everyone who has influence over anyone else in some situation, is a leader. The question is not, "Am I a leader?," it's "What kind of leader am I?"

So, to help us all figure out what kind of leader we are, I have a pop quiz for you. Here's a few leadership scenarios:

"A Whole New Kind of Hero"

Scenario #1

You are the leader of a growing parachurch ministry. One of your employees is not producing the kind of work needed for the ministry to thrive. You will:

a. Allow that employee the chance to work in someone else's ministry
b. Give the employee a three-month sabbatical to make them feel better
c. Empower the employee to perform better and keep them accountable
d. Call Dr. Paul Magnus (distinguished professor of leadership and management and member of the congregation)

Let's try Scenario #2:

You are a teacher in a Christian high school. You have a student who has fallen way behind the rest of the class. You will:

a. Suspend the student for not taking your class seriously
b. Tell the student they don't need to do any more work because you'll just pass them anyway
c. Sit down with the student to help them succeed
d. Call Paul Magnus

How about Scenario #3?

You own a restaurant and your main cook keeps calling in sick for no reason. You will:

a. Chase the cook out of your kitchen with a meat cleaver
b. Give the cook all they time off they want, no questions asked
c. Help the cook succeed in their job
d. Call Paul Magnus

Here's our problem when it comes to leading others: Either we overdo it and come on like dictators, or we underdo it, and look like overly-indulgent parents. I was in Tim Hortons this week and a group of five twelfth-grade guys sat at the table next to me. I knew they were in twelfth-grade because they were all talking about graduation coming up this weekend. There are certain things you expect to hear when five teenage guys are out together.

I heard something I didn't expect. They were all complaining how their parents were going overboard on their grad—clothes, parties, presents, the whole nine yards. They weren't respecting their parents because they were making it too easy for them. I was surprised, to say the least. We left at the same time. They all got into their new sports cars and I got into my ten-year-old Buick I bought for one dollar. Obviously, my parents hadn't gone overboard for my graduation.

I guess we've always had problems with leadership. We struggle with leadership just like we struggle with everything. The important thing is that God hasn't given up on us. No matter how bad we lead, God still has a card up his sleeve. He still leads us and shows us how to lead. That is what brings us to Isaiah's message this morning. God is showing us what he wants in a leader. He doesn't want a tyrant and he doesn't want some jolly big Santa Claus who just gives us whatever we want. What God wants in a leader is a servant. He tells us so in the very first verse. That kind of pops any kind of suspense right away—but there is still plenty we don't understand.

For starters, when God says, "Behold my servant," we don't really know who he's talking about. All kinds of people have been called the Lord's servant up to this point: Isaiah himself in chapter 20; Eliakim the servant of King Hezekiah in chapter 22; King David in chapter 37; and all of Israel or the faithful ones within the nation of Israel in chapter 41. Maybe you have your own guess as to who this servant is. We'll come back to that a bit later. What is obvious is that God isn't as interested in identifying this servant as he is describing what this servant is like. This is what God does for the first four verses—he talks about this servant. Let's see if he describes anyone we recognize.

This servant is strengthened or upheld by God, is chosen by God, loved by God, has God's Spirit upon him, is humble so he won't make a show of himself, and won't break bruised reeds or snuff out faintly burning wicks. (He'll be gentle with those who need it the most.)

What is most obvious is this servant is to bring justice to the whole world. Justice is mentioned three times here. That's no accident. This servant will establish justice. When you hear the word "justice," maybe your ears perked up. Everyone is talking about justice these days—those inside the church and those outside the church too. Everyone wants justice. But when most people use this word today, they mean something different than what Isaiah is talking about here. Today justice means that everyone is getting their own individual human rights. That sounds good until we try to

"A Whole New Kind of Hero"

figure out who gets to decide what those human rights are. Today, justice ends up being whatever we decide it is. This is a very horizontal view of justice—everyone is on the same level. The problem with this view is that justice is God's idea, not ours. Justice is vertical before it can be properly horizontal. We only understand justice when we see it on God's terms. Justice means that everything is working together in proper order—God is the one who decides what the proper order is because he's the one who created the order in the first place. Justice seems to go arm in arm with righteousness in the Old Testament, and righteousness means doing the right thing. Again, God is the one who shows us what those right things are. This is God's view of justice, not ours. This servant is to bring justice everywhere—to all the nations. So that means this servant will make it so the whole world is working just like it should. Our view of justice is "just us." God's view is "just him."

Any guesses who this servant might be?

All of a sudden, the text turns in a different direction. God goes from talking *about* his servant to talking *to* him. God turns from talking about the servant and talks more about himself—and what he will do for his servant.

Maybe something is starting to make a little more sense. The reason that the Lord's servant can accomplish all God says he will is because God is the one who is with this servant. What the servant does, he does because God is with him and gives him the power to do it. This is where God gives us part of his resume here: he is creator of both the heavens and the earth and all those who walk on the earth. He says, "I am the LORD; that is my name; my glory I give to no other, nor my praise to carved idols" (Isa 42:8). God is able to tell us what will happen in the future and the false gods and idols can't even tell us what has already happened.

So, it is God who makes it possible for this servant to be "a covenant for the people, a light to the nations." This servant will be the one who brings about all the blessings of being in covenant relationship with God—light to those who live in darkness, sight to those who are blind and release to those who are in prison.

I'm guessing, right about now, you think you've solved the mystery—you know who this servant is. We're in church, so the answer has to be: Jesus, right? The servant is Jesus. Well, yes and no.

Obviously, Jesus is the one who fulfills this servant role better than anyone, and the New Testament writers show us how Jesus does fulfill this role as the servant of Yahweh. But there is something more at play here. God doesn't tell us who he's talking about here on purpose, because God is always looking for servants like this. He wanted his people Israel to be his servants and they blew it; he wanted the kings of Israel, like David, to be his servants, but even David blew it—not to mention the rest of them. Jesus is the only one who didn't blow it. He is the ultimate servant of the Lord.

Here's the part we can't miss: God has found his perfect servant—Jesus—but that doesn't mean he has stopped looking for servants. Now that he has the perfect servant, this Jesus is able to make other servants. That's us. Our role is now to be servants. Obviously, we can't be servants like Jesus because Jesus never blew it—even once! But the good news is that Jesus has become a servant like us so we could be a servant like him.

I was building something in the backyard a few weeks ago. The lumber was all piled up there but before I could begin building I needed to get a pattern I could use to cut the rest of the pieces of lumber. This pattern had to be perfect—it had to be perfectly straight; it couldn't be knotty—it had to be just right. It took quite a few tries. The lumber always had something wrong with it—until I finally found the perfect pattern. When I found the pattern, then I could make others from it. This is what God had done with Jesus. He couldn't find a perfect servant anywhere else except in Jesus. But now in Jesus, God can make us into servants too. Servants help everyone see what life could be like if everything was like it was supposed to be—like it will be some day when Jesus returns to make it so.

That's what it means to be a leader. A leader is a servant. We lead by serving and we serve because Jesus was able to first serve us. And how do we know we are servants? When we don't care when people treat us like one.

"What Happens When God Colors Outside the Lines?"

Isaiah 44:24—45:13, ESV
June 21, 2015

Series Title: "The Fifth Gospel: Isaiah's Message for Us"

PRAYER FOR ILLUMINATION

LORD we acknowledge that you are sovereign which means you can act according to your own good purposes. But we confess that sometimes we just don't understand what you're up to and that turns us into a tailspin. Help us to act according to what we believe, and to trust you whether we understand you or not. And may the words of my mouth and the meditations of all our hearts be pleasing in your sight, O LORD, our Rock and our Redeemer. Amen.

SERMON

You never know what you're going get with a surprise—that's kind of the definition of a surprise, isn't it? But we know that some surprises are good, and some are not so good.

You apply for a job and hear back you are the top candidate for the job—good surprise. Then you find out they couldn't even bribe another person to apply for the job—bad surprise. You get a phone call saying you have just won an all-expenses paid trip—good surprise. Then you find out it's to Des Moines, Iowa—bad surprise. An angel reveals to you that there are golf courses in heaven—good surprise. Then he says you tee off tomorrow at 3:00 PM—bad surprise. Your surgeon informs you that he removed your kidney successfully and there were absolutely no complications—good surprise. Then you find out he removed the wrong one—bad surprise. The girl of your dreams says she'll go out to dinner with you—good surprise. Then she tells you she's bringing a date—bad surprise.

There is nothing more exhilarating than a good surprise and nothing more aggravating than a bad one. But whether it's a good or bad one, all surprises have one thing in common—they mess with our tidy little worlds. They are by nature unexpected and so they force us to adjust our lives. Sometimes that can push us over the edge. We like to think we have everything under control—we are all control freaks when it comes to what we expect.

If you have been following Jesus for very long, you have probably been surprised before. That just seems to go along with the territory. As a matter of fact, part of what it means to grow as a Christ follower is to learn how to respond when God seems to come out of left field on you. If you want to know how you're doing in your Christian growth, you might ask yourself, "How do I handle it when God surprises me, when he colors outside the lines?"

We see all this in action this morning. God's people need him. If he does not send a deliverer, they won't be delivered. God has been promising them deliverance but hasn't really told them how he's going to do it. This morning he tells them and that's when all the commotion begins. So, in many ways, this passage is a case study in surprise. It has a beginning, a middle, and an end—just like any good story.

This story begins with God. That's where all stories begin, whether we admit it or not. It is important to know that God is always the main character—he's the protagonist—not us. Most of our problems come from getting this wrong. If we think the story is all about us, then we are bound for an unhappy ending. As a matter of fact, this whole story, which has three main parts, is about God because God is the only one talking here from beginning to end.

God starts by introducing himself. There are three things he wants his people to know about him. First, he is their Redeemer or deliverer: "Thus says the LORD, your Redeemer" (Isa 44:24a). If his people are to be delivered, he is the one to do it. But not only is he their Redeemer, he's the Creator—not just creating them but creating everything. We've seen that God's role as Creator is the foundation of his authority—he made it all, it's all his. He didn't need help to do it either: "I am the LORD, who made all things, who *alone* stretched out the heavens, who spread out the

"What Happens When God Colors Outside the Lines?"

earth *by myself.*" And even beyond that, God is the one who watches over all he has created. He is Redeemer, Creator and sustainer. He makes those who oppose him look like idiots, and he confirms the words of his own servants. He is the one who dried up the Red Sea, so they could cross on dry ground. He is the one who promises that Jerusalem and their temple will be rebuilt. And here's the kicker—he's the one who is going to choose the pagan Persian king Cyrus to do the delivering of his people. Up to this point, all his people are with him, shouting the odd "amen"—until they hear the C-word—Cyrus.

They never saw that coming. It's bad enough to be overrun by pagans—like the Assyrians and the Babylonians—but to be saved by a pagan? How could God do this? We can see them squinting and adjusting their hearing aids. But God just drops the bombshell and leaves them standing there. He's just told them who he is and what he's going to do and then he turns to speak to Cyrus himself. In the first section, God explains *what* he's going to do, but now in the second part, he's going to tell us *why*.

If the first few verses would have been hard to hear for God's own people, these next ones are even worse. God refers to Cyrus here as his anointed—that's the word for messiah! God is talking to this pagan king like he is Israel's messiah. As surprises go, this one is way off the charts. It is unthinkable.

God goes on to pledge what he's going to do for Cyrus: he has taken him by the hand and he will deliver kings and nations to him; he will give him amazing success and will give him untold treasure. By this time, we might suspect that God is just rubbing it in—but he's not. He is doing all this for a reason. Actually, three reasons, and he spells them all out in this center section.

God is doing all this for Cyrus so "that you [Cyrus] may know that it is I, the LORD, the God of Israel, who call you by your name" (Isa 45:3). God chooses to work through Cyrus so that this pagan king knows it is Yahweh who has commissioned him. And we see this fulfilled in the book of Ezra in the very first year of Cyrus' reign as he sends a proclamation throughout his entire kingdom saying, "Thus says Cyrus king of Persia: the LORD [Yahweh], the God of heaven, has given me all the kingdoms of the earth, and he has charged me to build him a house at Jerusalem, which is in Judah" (Ezra 1:2). The first reason God works through Cyrus is so that Cyrus himself knows who is behind all this effort to rebuild Jerusalem and the temple.

This does not mean that Cyrus is converted—because lots of pagan kings, including Pharaoh, had to acknowledge God without believing in him.

But informing Cyrus himself about what he's up to is just the tip of the iceberg for God. His second reason is found in verses 4 and 5. He chooses Cyrus not just so Cyrus will know Yahweh is delivering his people, but also that through choosing Cyrus, his own people will know that he is the LORD and there is no other. Listen to these verses: "For the sake of my servant Jacob, and Israel my chosen, I call you by your name, I name you though you do not know me. I am the LORD, and there is no other, besides me there is no God; I equip you, though you do not know me."

Twice, Yahweh mentions that Cyrus doesn't even know him. But that's not the issue. God is going to use him anyway. It's not the first time and won't be the last when God uses someone to accomplish his purposes and that person is none the wiser for it. Why God uses Cyrus is so that all Israel will know he is the LORD and there is no God but him. Cyrus doesn't have to know Yahweh is Redeemer, but God's people do. God is working this out for his own people's benefit—whether they know that or not. Sometimes we don't understand that God has been at work in some surprising way in our lives until after it's happened. It's like Peter in the book of Acts. He's locked up in the inner cell chained to two guards. He's about to be executed in the morning, but in the middle of the night an angel comes and wakes him up and escorts him right out of the prison. The chains fall off and the prison doors open, just like leaving Real Canadian Superstore, and Peter is out in the middle of the street before he realizes what has happened. See, Cyrus doesn't have to know but eventually Israel does. Cyrus can be an unwitting witness, but Israel has to know.

God's not done. He chooses Cyrus for a third reason: "that people may know, from the rising of the sun and from the west, that there is no one besides me; I am the LORD, and there is no other" (v. 6). God chooses Cyrus so that everyone knows that he is the LORD and there is no other. So, obviously, God has his reasons for working in this surprising way. What remains to be seen is how Israel deals with this surprise.

It doesn't look like they are taking it very well because, in the third part of our text (vv. 9–10), God says to them: "Woe to him who strives with him who formed him, a pot among earthen pots! Does the clay say to him that forms it, 'What are you making' or 'Your work has no handles'? Woe to him who says to a father, 'What are you begetting?' or to a woman, 'With what are you in labor?'"

"What Happens When God Colors Outside the Lines?"

The news of God's plan to deliver them has not gone over well and God's own people are challenging God's ability to make this call. It's just too surprising to them. They can't get their heads around it.

So, what does God do? Does he say, "Oh, I'm sorry I didn't consult with you first. Let me come up with plan B"? No, he reminds his own people who they are. They are just pots, not potters; they are tots, not parents. Then he reminds them who he is—because (apparently) they have bad short-term memories. He is the Creator and he will use Cyrus to set them free and rebuild their city. End of discussion. And God does use Cyrus to deliver his people. And that's that.

Isn't it a shame when God's own people won't trust him? His surprises remind us that he is God and God alone. His surprises are our salvation. They remind us that our God is entirely faithful, but he is completely unpredictable,

Maybe you came here this morning with no expectation of being surprised. Maybe you like having everything perfectly predictable—just the way you like it. The problem with that kind of worship, or that kind of life, is that *we're* in control of it and not God. God is a God of surprises. He surprised Abraham and Sarah with a baby in their sunset years. He conquered Jericho by surround sound; he made Gideon defeat the Midianites with a bunch of crack pots and trumpets; he chose little old Israel from among all the nations of the earth; he delivered them through the Red Sea on dry land; he sent his only Son into the political backwaters of Palestine; he let sinful people nail his Son to the cross for our sins; and surprise of surprises (at least for Satan), he raised his Son from the dead three days later. God is a God of surprises. We had better just get used to it. We haven't worshipped until we've been surprised.

So, what surprise does Jesus have for you today? Is your God one who always colors inside the lines? Did you come to worship this morning with absolutely no expectation of hearing something you haven't heard before, something that might rearrange your tidy little world? Maybe you're not just listening closely enough to what God is telling us here. Because the very moment we think we have it all figured out—*surprise!*

"Extreme Makeover: David's House Edition"

Amos 9:11-15, ESV
January 21, 2018

Series Title: "God Talk: Major Themes from the Minor Prophets"

PRAYER FOR ILLUMINATION

LORD we come amazed at two things this morning: your continuous, gracious love for us and our own stubborn tendency to take this love for granted and go our own ways. We know it should be different, and deep down, we want it to be. We come here eagerly wanting you to show us how. So, may the words of my mouth and the meditations of all our hearts be pleasing in your sight, O LORD, our Rock and our Redeemer. Amen.

SERMON

Where are all our farm people today? If you were raised on a farm, raise your hand. I'm proud to say I'm a farm boy, and I married a girl raised on a farm. My father was a farmer and so was my grandfather and my great-grandfather.

If you were raised on a farm, chances are you look at life differently, because farm life is different. Farmers tend to stand out from the rest of the crowd. So, how do you know if you're a farmer?

You might be a farmer if:

- your tractor is worth six times more than your pickup truck
- your idea of a social event is an auction sale
- every vehicle you own smells a bit like cow manure

"Extreme Makeover: David's House Edition"

- your dog rides in your truck more than your spouse
- you have a strong brand loyalty when it comes to farm equipment
- you have never thrown away a five-gallon pail
- you have a different free hat to wear for each occasion
- you've driven off the road looking at your neighbor's crop
- you learned to drive before you could see over the dashboard

That's how it is when you're from the farm. Not everyone else appreciates this. Maybe you knew this already, but one of the minor prophets was a farmer. Amos was a farmer from the hill country of the Southern Kingdom of Judah. He didn't go to prophet's school, he didn't hang out with other prophets—he hung out with sheep and sycamore trees. God called him to go and prophesy against the Northern Kingdom of Israel almost eight centuries before Jesus was born.

You can well imagine how that went over—this untrained guy from the southern hills coming up against King Jeroboam II of Israel and his corrupt administration. In a situation like that, you'd think Amos would talk softly and carry a little stick. Not Amos—he screams loudly and carries a big stick. For more than eight chapters he blasts their injustice, affluence and their superficial worship. He delivers spoken oracles and sees visions—and they all have one common theme: *woe* to you!

The nation of Israel is unaware that disaster is around the corner; they are complacent and affluent—the rich are oppressing the poor and feel that's fine as long as they show up to worship. Amos is an equal opportunity prophet, and he even blasts the women of Israel calling them, "cows of Bashan" (Amos 4:1). It's like a farmer from Hanley going down to Hollywood, walking up to the Kardashians and saying, "Woe to you, heifers of Hollywood!"

We read through Amos' book and we get used to hearing bad news—until the last five verses. All this bad news, and then, at the end, finally some good news. What is with that? Many scholars doubt these verses come from Amos because they seem out of character from the rest of the book. But they are the very reason for the whole book. It turns out Amos is a preacher of both hell fire *and* hope.

For over eight chapters, Amos is calling Israel to repent and now he shows they why they should. After all this destruction and judgment will come restoration.

Last week we looked at two important themes for the prophets: covenant—a binding agreement with stipulations and consequences—and the day of the Lord—the time when God shows up and acts in powerful ways. Both these themes are important in our text from Amos. God uses covenant talk to his people here—he calls himself the LORD, your God. That's covenant language. It's how God identifies himself when he is talking about his covenant relationship with Israel. He also makes reference to "that day" in verse 11 and "the days are coming" in verse 13—that is the day of the Lord language. This means God is referring to a time when he will act in a powerful way in relation to his people Israel. But most of all, Amos introduces us to another key theme: restoration. Restoration is God's promise to re-establish his purposes and peace to his people.

So, what is Amos saying? He's saying God will makes things new. That is the ultimate good news when we are almost getting used to the bad news. Restoration is the promise to make things new.

Amos fills in the blanks as to what this means. It means the new is way better than the old. That seems like a bit of a no-brainer, but we shouldn't ignore it. God goes into great detail to give us a picture of what this new life is going to be like in terms that Israelites in the eighth century before Christ would understand: "The days are coming when the plowman shall overtake the reaper" (Amos 9:13). In other words, when God brings in the new, the land will be so productive that we won't be able to get the combines off the field before it is time to bring out the seeders for the new crop to be planted. And look at those terraced vineyards on all the hills. The grape crop will be so plentiful, the hills will look like one of those punch fountains with wine pouring over from one level to the other, all the way down. We'll barely get the grape seeds in the ground before the wine presses are filled with people up to their eyeballs in grapes.

In that day, we will have no worries about being dragged off into exile or being under the thumb of some foreign power. We will be in control and in our land forever.

The whole idea of being in their precious land forever was a foundational part of their hope. To them, heaven was being right there in their homeland. This is pretty exciting to me because in a couple of weeks, Peggy and I and two of our kids will be heading to Israel for ten days. I haven't been there for nearly forty years, but I still remember how sacred the land is to Israelis—maybe that's why they call it the Holy Land.

That was what they thought at that time. I'm not so sure my idea of heaven is to come back to Saskatchewan forever. Our family moved back here from Prince Edward Island because God called us here, not for the weather or the scenery, and not because we thought this was heaven.

"Extreme Makeover: David's House Edition"

But Amos also reminds us the new comes out of the old. Before we start thinking there is no use for the old, or the old doesn't matter at all, God reminds us his work of salvation is a work of restoration and not complete innovation. God starts with what he has already created and then restores and improves it to the point we are utterly amazed. Amos' audience gets all this naturally—it's part of their theology. We need a little help and thankfully we get some help from our English translation here. The translators use "re" words like: repair, rebuild, and restore.

God re-creates what he has already created. He is the cosmic recycler. He is going to take King David's broken-down, old tent, and he's going to give it a renovation that will blow our minds.

It's bit like that TV show from a few years back, *Extreme Makeover: Home Edition*. Remember that? The host was a rather annoying guy called Ty Pennington. They would find a poorer family living in a ramshackled house. They would send the family away and then give the house such a makeover that it would take your breath away. At the end of the show they would bring the family back, but they would hide the house behind the show's huge bus. At the climax of the show, Ty would say, "Bus driver, move that bus!" Then the family would see their renovated home. They would scream, laugh, cry, fall on the ground, and go running through the house—they were overjoyed.

Amos reminds us those old hopes and dreams we thought were dead and gone will one day be revitalized and renewed beyond our wildest imagination. In our day, when we are flooded with innovations but starved in our imaginations, this is good news indeed.

God is still taking the old and making things new. As a matter of fact, back in the early years of the church, Amos' words came back in a way that saved the day and made it so that all of us could be part of the church today. For the first years of the church, they felt Jesus just came to save Jewish people, and if people wanted to become part of the church, they had to become Jewish first. If that teaching won the day, we would probably not be part of this church today. But as the church meets in Jerusalem to discuss this issue, it is James who quotes this very passage from Amos and says, "God is making something new. He is taking the old tent of David that was only for the Jewish people and he is making it into a dwelling place for all nations to come in faith."

God is making things new. He's not finished yet either.

Neither is Amos done. If we look at our text in light of all that Amos has said, we realize the new is only for those who are made new. That, in the end, is Amos' message.

He's spent over eight chapters trying to get Israel to return to God, even when he tells them what is going to happen to them if they don't. But now Amos is telling us what will happen when they do return to God.

Israel doesn't return to God and their nation is overrun and obliterated by the Assyrians. The surprising thing is that God doesn't give up on his people just because they give up on him. Out of his amazing mercy and grace God promises a time when he will still make things new. This isn't something we earn by our repentance or our goodness. This is something that comes out of God's grace. We don't deserve it and yet he still gives it to us.

Israel wasn't going to be able to experience this restoration because they didn't want to be made new themselves. They were satisfied with the way they were. They were fine with being oppressive to the poor, self-sufficient, entitled, and going through the motions in worship. The truth is, unless we are made new, we can't enjoy the new—it's just too weird for us. We will never fit. I've had all kinds of people say to me, "Why would I want to go to heaven? I wouldn't have any fun there anyway. I'd be bored. I'd rather be in hell with all my friends having a good time." Guess what? They are probably right. You can't live a renewed life without a renewed heart.

There is a well-quoted part of C. S. Lewis' book *The Weight of Glory* where he writes: "It would seem that our Lord finds our desires not too strong, but too weak. We are half-hearted creatures, fooling about with drink and sex and ambition when infinite joy is offered us, like an ignorant child who wants to go on making mud pies in a slum because he cannot imagine what is meant by the offer of a holiday at the sea. We are far too easily pleased."

Amos' words cry out for our response. There are all kinds of ways these words can apply to us.

Do we really want God to make all things new? It always starts with what God does first—then we are called to respond.

What difference would it make in how we approached each other?
In how we approached worshipping God?
In how we approached our First Nations brothers and sisters?
The list could go on.

There is one thing these questions have in common: They all require us to do something. They call to us to get off our seats and act. They shout, "People of God, move those butts!"

"Why Do You Reject Our Worship?"

Malachi 2:10–16, ESV

May 26, 2013

Series Title: "God's Answers to Our Questions"

PRAYER FOR ILLUMINATION

LORD, there is nothing we want to do more than worship you with clean hands and pure hearts. It is what you have made us to do, yet we find all kinds of ways to mess it up. We can be the weakest at what makes us strong, we're the poorest at what makes us rich. So, help us to worship you with all we have and all we are. And may the words of my mouth and the meditations of all our hearts be pleasing in your sight, O LORD, our Rock and our Redeemer. Amen.

SERMON

It can be hard for introverts to learn how to worship. I know this to be true because I "are" one. Every personality test I take, I get the same result—I am, whether I like it or not, an introvert. You might be thinking, "Man are you ever in the wrong job!" Sometimes I think that too. It is important to remember, however, that statistically speaking, there are more pastors who are introverts than extroverts. I mention this only because that's probably a common misconception.

    I grew up in a church where it was safe to be an introvert. I was raised in a church that thought Presbyterians were way too emotional in worship. You didn't move when you were worshipping at our church unless you were having a seizure. If you just held your hands out perpendicular to your body, we all thought you were getting ready to handle snakes. You just stood there, frozen, so you didn't draw attention to yourself. I remember one Sunday—a lady fainted right in the middle of the worship service. It was serious enough they had to call the ambulance. We all freaked out, not because this lady was obviously ill, but because she had the audacity to make a spectacle of herself in the middle of worship. I remember looking down my nose at her as they wheeled her out on the stretcher and saying, "Really? Mom!"

Then I moved away from home and realized maybe that wasn't the way it was everywhere else. I slowly learned I didn't necessarily have to be part of the frozen chosen—I could be part of the thawed squad. I'm not trying to make you use your hands in worship if you don't want to or to make you feel embarrassed if you do. That's not my point. More importantly, worship is not so much a matter of how little or how much you move your hands or whole bodies. Worship is much deeper than that.

But before we get to that, we need to recap where we've been since we've started looking at the book of Malachi. If we don't get this progression, we don't get what Malachi is saying to us. Remember Malachi was a prophet in Israel after they had returned from captivity in Babylon. They had rebuilt the temple, but life for them had flattened out, was tasteless, because life was not living up to their expectations. They felt God wasn't holding up his end of the deal, and so they became disillusioned and cynical about life in general and God in particular. They have these "in your face" questions to ask God and God is in the act of giving them answers. And as is often the case when we ask God questions, we don't always get the answers we wanted or even expected. So, prepare to be surprised yet again.

Two weeks ago, we found out that God shows his love for his people by choosing them to be his people. We learned a bit about God's choice, or his election of us as his people. That made us a bit nervous. Then last week, we added a piece to the puzzle. God shows his love to us by choosing us to be his people, and we, as his people, show our love to him by worshipping him alone as our God. Last week we learned a little bit about a covenant relationship. That whole idea of covenant is important for this morning and the rest of the book of Malachi.

So, this morning we add another piece. Worshipping God starts with who we are before it moves to what we do. We can't jump over the part of who we are and go straight to what we do. If our "doing" doesn't come out of our "being", we can fake it and try to look good on the outside when we're

"Why Do You Reject Our Worship?"

not so good on the inside. So that's what we'll look at today: worshipping God starts with who we are before it moves to what we do.

The people ask God, "Why are you rejecting our worship?," or in other words, "Why are you not blessing us when we show up and worship our faces off every week?" God's answer is pretty simple: I reject worship from my people when it is just an outward show and doesn't reflect the true condition of their hearts. In God's words—he says his people are faithless. He repeats this same word five times. To act faithlessly or treacherously or deceptively is a covenant term. It is used when people want to make it look like they are being faithful to the covenant, but it's just a cover-up or a pretense. The word actually comes from the word for "clothing." This was the rough outer garment people would wear over everything—a cloak, really. That's a good way to describe it, because faithless people were trying to cover, or cloak, their rebellious and selfish hearts with something that hid the truth about them. These people were putting on a good show when they brought their sacrifices to the temple—covering the altar with tears, weeping, and groaning—acting like it was all God's fault that they weren't getting what they wanted.

God is very specific in what he is using as a measuring stick for their faithlessness. He is using their approach to marriage—how they treat their spouses has a huge impact on how God treats them. That is what makes them faithless.

Malachi draws our attention to two different issues about marriage that show faithlessness. The first is found in verses 10-12 and deals with the Israelites intermarrying with the pagans. This sounds not only old-fashioned but bigoted. Is God completely against interracial marriage? No, he isn't. Malachi is not talking about race but about religion. It has to do with Israel's covenant with God. They were to remain pure as God's people and worship God alone. What happened when God's people married those outside of Israel? These spouses brought the worship of their own gods into the household and that just led to trouble. That happened over and over again in Israel's history—even to wise King Solomon. In 1 Kings 11:4 it says, "For when Solomon was old his wives turned away his heart after other gods, and his heart was not wholly true to the LORD his God, as was the heart of David his father." Part of Israel's commitment to their one God and Father was to remain one pure people, completely devoted to worshipping God and God alone.

To marry pagan spouses was to do the same thing as the priests did to God's altar when they offered defective animals as sacrifices—remember that from last week? These priests profaned the altar by that kind of disrespect. Now anyone in Israel who married a pagan was doing the exact same thing to the covenant and to what God considered to be holy. The same word is being used here.

You can't despise or profane God's covenant and then show up for worship and try to act like nothing's wrong, like it's business as usual. As a matter of fact, God says those kinds of people will be cut off from his people. That is not good news for those who should know what it is they're missing. To go from being God's child to being his enemy is not a promotion. To be excluded from God's people is like being sent away from Thanksgiving dinner for bad behavior. You know what you're missing.

This is not the only way Israel was showing their faithlessness. In verses 13–16, Malachi says their second issue was divorce. Apparently, what was happening was that guys were divorcing their Hebrew wives and then marrying pagan ones because that would open up larger business networks for them.

If marrying pagans was a violation of their covenant with God, divorcing their wives of many years was a violation of the covenant they had with their wives. It is this same one God and Father who was in covenant relationship with all Israel who made husband and wife into one—making them unified at the deepest level of their lives. He made them one, so their children would be godly—aware of this one true God.

This is a beautiful picture of God's intention for marriage—God has made husband and wife one—through and through. No one can just throw that away to make more money or meet his own goals that serve his own agenda. God hates that kind of action because it violently rips apart what he has put together. It violates the covenant relationship we have with God, and the covenant we have with our mate; it affects the raising of godly children.

So, God says you can't come to worship and make a big show of it all when you're hiding this kind of heart—one that is more focused on yourself than on God or those closest to you. No amount of worship calisthenics can cover that up. The issue remains: worship starts with who we are, not with what we do. If we start with what we do, we can fool ourselves into thinking God owes us something. He doesn't.

The truth is, we can't hide anything from God. Ask Adam and Eve. After they ate the fruit from the tree of the knowledge of good and evil, they

"Why Do You Reject Our Worship?"

realized they were naked, and they felt shame for the first time. So, instead of talking with God in the cool of the evening, they thought they could hide from God. Not a great idea. Have you ever tried to play hide-and-seek with one who sees all things, knows all things, and is everywhere? God comes along and plays with Adam a bit. He calls out, "Where are you?" Then good old Adam, just like a two-year-old, blows it and speaks up, "I heard you coming, and I was afraid because I was naked." No matter how hard we try, we can't hide anything from God. God can't be fooled. We can fool each other, but nobody cons God. But even though he knows us through and through, God still comes looking for us. He wants to find us; he wants to talk with us; he wants to hang out with us.

Here's the good news: Through Christ he has found us, and he does talk with us. What he asks in return is for us to be honest and open in our worship. He tells us what he told the Samaritan woman: "God is spirit and those who worship him, must worship in spirit and truth" (John 4:23). This starts with who we are and then moves on to what we do. Worship starts in our head and heart and works its way through to our hands and feet—it even goes through our wallets on the way down. Our worship is not about our passion or our posture—it's about our parentage. God is our Father, and he deserves every last part of us in worship. And with God's help, this we will do.

"How Are We Robbing You?"

Malachi 3:6–12, ESV

June 9, 2013

Series Title: "God's Answers to Our Questions"

PRAYER FOR ILLUMINATION

LORD, we want to honor you with all we are and all we've got and all we've been given. You have been so gracious and faithful to us and we want our lives to overflow in grateful worship to you. Save us from the selfishness that refuses to experience your grace. And may the words of my mouth and the meditations of all our hearts be pleasing in your sight, O LORD, our Rock and our Redeemer. Amen.

SERMON

Maybe you've had one of those experiences when you were expecting one thing and actually received something else, something completely unexpected. Maybe you are dreading going to the dentist because you thought you had lots of cavities. But you go, and your teeth are perfect—no drilling and spitting blood, and you get a free toothbrush. Or maybe you're an eighth grade student and were expecting your trip on the Cabot Trail to be very boring, but you went and had a great time. (Please tell my kids.)

    I remember several years ago, getting ready to defend my thesis. Normally, these are times when several learned people gather in a room and try to find all the possible reasons why you can't graduate. Imagine my surprise when I actually had fun; at the end I wasn't fielding questions but telling jokes. Who knew?

"How Are We Robbing You?"

Have you ever had experiences like that? I had one of those this week as I was looking at this passage from Malachi. You might have noticed that Malachi has some more strong words for us here—that's not the unexpected part. We've heard his challenging words for several weeks in a row now and we've grown to expect that. That's what prophets do—they talk smack. But this time he mentions tithing, and that can make us all nervous. You're probably nervous, because you're thinking to yourself, "Here comes another sermon on giving—a sermon on the amount." This usually means we're way behind on the budget or the preacher has had a bad week. But neither of these is true—this time. These sermons make preachers nervous too, because we know what you're thinking.

Imagine my surprise when I realized this text isn't really about tithing at all. That's not Malachi's main point in this text. As a matter of fact, we have used this text to prove a lot of things over the years, but none of them really is the main message of this passage.

Let's pull a few of these weeds before we get down to Malachi's message. The passage begins with, "I the Lord do not change" (Mal 3:6a). Many say this text teaches that God is unchangeable, or as the theologians call it—immutable. The problem with this is it rips this statement from its context and makes it sound like we have freeze-dried God, that he is frozen in time and doesn't change or decay—he always is just the same. That sounds pretty static and abstract. It makes our personal God look very impersonal. Malachi is actually saying God shows he doesn't change by staying faithful to the covenant relationship he's made with his people. His people may waver and wander, but he never does. And that's the only hope we have as his people. He's not moody or selfish or flighty or easily bored like we can be. It's his unchanging faithfulness that keeps us from being consumed.

We also use this text to teach about tithing. That is not its main point either. We'll find that out in a minute.

Others use this passage to teach what we call the prosperity gospel: God wants us to be rich, and if we just give to him then God will automatically give riches back to us in abundance. All we have to do is "name it and claim it," and it's ours. This misses Malachi's point completely. There is no such thing as "name it and claim it" in the Bible—there's just "live it and give it." The prosperity gospel is no gospel at all—it's spiritual pornography—a dangerous counterfeit of the real thing.

So, what is Malachi talking about anyway? If it is none of these three things, what is it? This passage is a call to repentance, a call for God's people to return to him. and everything else flows out from this. It's not so much about tithing as it is about turning—turning back to God in repentance. It's not so much about giving as it is about loving—if we love God greatly, we will give generously to him.

Remember in Malachi's day, God's people had grown cold in their relationship with God. Their lives were blah and tasteless and they were blaming God for it. They were going through the motions; their hearts were anywhere else than with God.

Guess what? God wants his people back. He always does. That's what is unchangeable about God. When God makes a covenant relationship with his people, he plays for keeps, he signs it in blood, and he never stops wanting us back when we wander away or rebel against him.

That's why God says what he says at the beginning of this passage. He says, "For I the LORD do not change; therefore you, O children of Jacob are not consumed. From the days of your fathers you have turned aside from my statutes and have not kept them" (Mal 3:6, 7a). He reminds his people that both he and they have hearts with a history. His heart has remained the same and theirs has been wandering since the beginning.

That's why God says, "Return to me and I will return to you" (Mal 3:7b). This is a call to repent, to turn around from the way we're living right now and to be faithful to the God who has made us his own. This is God calling his own people to be true to their promises to God because he has always been true to his.

The problem is that his people are so jaded here that they don't even know they need to repent. Here's where the giving the tithe part comes in. God answers their question "How shall we return (or repent)?" by saying, "You can start by not robbing me or ripping me off."

They reply, "And just how are we robbing you?"

"By the way you give back to me."

Here's how repentance relates to giving. The way we show God that we love him back, instead of just loving ourselves, is to be generous in what we give to him. The fact that God's people were stingy and cheap with God showed they really didn't love him, and they didn't appreciate all God had done for them. When we're cheap with God, we cheat God, because we're cheating on God (with ourselves).

In Malachi's time, God's people were cursed because of their stinginess. This only makes sense if we understand how this covenant relationship was made in the first place. Back in Deuteronomy 28, Moses is reminding the nation of Israel about this covenant agreement.

> And if you faithfully obey the voice of the LORD your God, being careful to do all his commandments that I command you today, the LORD your God will set you high above all the nations of the earth. And all these blessings shall come upon you and overtake you, if you obey the voice of the LORD your God. . .. But if you will not obey the voice of the LORD your God or be careful to do all his commandments and his statutes that I command you today, then all these curses shall come upon you and overtake you" (1,2,15).

God's people were miserable because they were miserly with God. They hadn't been faithful to the covenant and were experiencing the curses instead of the blessings.

So, this is God's challenge: Bring in the full tithe to the temple treasury and stop trying to get away with as little as possible. That is what shows a heart that has returned to God and is showing love and gratitude to him. Back under Israel's covenant agreement with God, they were to give three tithes or offerings: one was a tenth given to the Levites because they had no land of their own; another was a giving of a tenth of all the produce of the land, and then there was a great feast when everyone brought this to the temple—like a huge harvest party or Thanksgiving dinner; the third tithe was taken every three years and it was to care for the poor. These tithes and offerings were there to remind God's people that everything they had was from God, and it was a way to care for one another as well.

To be cheap with God this way was closing up your heart to God and to others in need. So, God raises the stakes by daring his people to repent. He says, "If you come back to me, and show your love through being obedient and generous, you will see that I've been faithful all along. I'm just waiting to flood you with the blessings I've promised you as part of our covenant relationship." When God says "flood," he means "flood." God says he'll open the windows of heaven, which is the same phrase he used to describe the great flood back in Noah's day.

Not only does God promise to pour out these blessings, he also promises to reverse the curses they are experiencing. No more crop failures. God will take care of the pests that are devouring all their food—that probably means locusts (or teenagers). "Then all the nations will call you blessed, for you will be a land of delight," just like I promised you back in Deuteronomy 28.

Wouldn't you want to come back to a God like that? We all would, I'm sure. But the question is: Have we come back to him? Malachi shows us how we can tell. If we are stingy toward God, our hearts have still not opened up to his faithful love—they have remained closed up and dry. Not only does that show contempt to God, but it harms others and even ourselves.

You may have noticed the recent advertising campaign by Visa asking us if we "*smallenfreuden.*" This strange word is a combination of the English word for "small" and the German word for "joy"—*fruede*. It's the joy of small. Visa is trying to get us to use our credit cards for even the smallest of purchases. Is there really joy in using credit to buy a Timbit? What's joyful about thinking so small?

Luke tells the story about how Simon the Pharisee invites Jesus to dinner and the town floosy crashes the party by pouring this expensive perfume all over Jesus' feet. Simon is so tight, he doesn't even spring for a basin of water to wash Jesus' feet. Jesus ends up telling Simon, "Therefore I tell you, her sins, which are many, are forgiven—for she loved much. But he who is forgiven little, loves little" (Luke 7:47). We could also say, "The one who is forgiven little, gives little."

No matter what it is we can give: money, time, service, or whatever, this is how we show our love to Jesus for what he has already done for us. The apostle Paul puts it this way: "For you know the grace of our Lord Jesus Christ, that tough he was rich, yet for your sake he became poor, so that you by his poverty might become rich" (2 Cor 8:9). Is this the kind of Lord you can *smallenfreuden*?

3

Preaching Narrative Biblical Texts

MORE THAN HALF OF the Bible is in narrative form. Despite this fact, many preachers do not know how to preach a narrative text. Often narratives have been turned into moralistic fables where the congregation is urged to emulate the actions of the main character in the text. Some sermons ramble all over the place trying to piece together a complete biography of a biblical character. That hardly does justice to the respective texts from which the episodes are taken. Other sermons on narrative texts mention a verse or two from the story, draw a contemporary application, or mention some "timeless" truth, then continue repeating the process several times before the narrative is over and the congregation is completely confused or overloaded or both.

Narrative texts communicate in a more indirect fashion. The author makes decisions in crafting the story. The storyteller uses setting, plot, character development, dialogue, point of view, and other narrative devices as tools of the trade. The narrative paints a picture of a world that teaches a lesson and draws us into some kind of response in light of this picture. Most narratives have an inductive flow and only divulge their intended impact near the very end. Narratives are found throughout the Bible—in the Pentateuch, Former Prophets (some sections in the Latter Prophets), Gospels, and Acts of the Apostles. Some of them are lengthy and involved, comprised of several shorter stories or episodes, and some are short fictional stories such as Jesus' parables.

Preaching challenges in the narrative genres include: reinforcing the understanding that constructed stories do not mean they are not relating the truth (stories are a way of telling the truth rather than make-believe); making the sermons too pointed and turning them into moralistic tales; or making them so polyvalent and pointless that the congregation leaves entertained but not engaged.

"Why Did God Test Abraham?"

Genesis 22:1–19, ESV
February 5, 2017

Series Title: "Have You Ever Wondered Why?"

PRAYER FOR ILLUMINATION

LORD, you are holy and mighty. You are loving and forgiving. Knowing all this, we still feel we need to take control of our own lives; the results are always disastrous. Help us to see you for who you are. Help us to see ourselves for who we are. Help us never to confuse our ways with your ways. And forgive us when we do. And may the words of my mouth and the meditations of all our hearts be pleasing in your sight, O LORD, our Rock and our Redeemer. Amen.

SERMON

There are dangerous places out there—we all know that. We know it's dangerous when we find ourselves between a mother bear and her cub, or between a hockey player and the boards, or between a teenager and their cell phone. The two most dangerous places for me (if you don't count being stranded out in the Atlantic Ocean in a canoe—another story for another time) would be a bookstore and Home Depot. Bookstores are dangerous because I am tempted to spend too much money. Home Depot is dangerous because it taunts me into doing things I shouldn't be doing. Here's how they do it: they flash three letters in front of my face—DIY—do it yourself. There are a thousand ways for me to hurt myself just by taking that advice.

Sledge hammers and power tools are dangerous for me and for all those around me. For me, DIY actually means don't injure yourself.

Actually, do it yourself is dangerous for all of us. When we are faced with a problem or a challenge, what is often our first response? What can I do to get myself out of this situation? That's DIY.

When we look at ourselves and don't like what we see, how are we tempted to think? I'll just find ways to make myself better. That's DIY.

When somebody does something nasty to us—how do we respond? I'll just do something worse back to them. That's DIY.

So, DIY is an issue for all of us at one time or another. I know it is an issue for Abraham.

Last week we saw the first time God spoke to Abraham and now today we look at the thirty-fifth and final time God speaks to him, and it's a doozy. Back in chapter 12 when God first speaks to Abram, Abram listens and obeys. After that, it can be a bit of a toss-up.

Before chapter 12 is over, Abram leaves the land of promise looking for food and tries to tell Pharaoh that Sarai is his sister to save his own skin. DIY.

Later in chapter 15, God promises Abram that his offspring will be as plentiful as the stars. "And he believed the LORD, and he counted it to him as righteousness." Here, he trusts in the Lord.

Then in chapter 16, Sarai has had enough. Still no baby in sight and so she tells Abram to sleep with her slave Hagar, and Ishmael is born. DIY.

In chapter 18, after his name change to Abraham (father of a multitude), the Lord tells him they will have a baby within the year; Sarah (princess) overhears and laughs to herself—yeah, right. DIY. God knows that even if there's snow on the roof, there can be fire in the furnace!

Chapter 20—Abraham tries to pass off Sarah as his sister again, this time to King Abimelech. DIY.

In chapter 21, Isaac is born, just as God promised back in chapter 18. Isaac means "laughter," because Sarah says, "God has made laughter for me; everyone who hears will laugh over me . . . Who would have said to Abraham that Sarah would nurse children? Yet I have borne him a son in his old age" (Gen 21:6, 7). Back to trusting God.

By the time we get to chapter 22, we're not sure which Abraham is going to show up. So, this story begins: "After these things God tested Abraham and said to him, 'Abraham!' And he said, 'Here am I.' He said, 'Take your son, your only son Isaac, whom you love, and go to the land of

"Why Did God Test Abraham?"

Moriah, and offer him there as a burnt offering on one of the mountains of which I will tell you'" (Genesis 22:2).

We hear these words differently than Abraham did. Right from the get-go, we are told this is just a test—God really doesn't want Abraham to kill Isaac, to kill his "laughter." But Abraham doesn't know it's a test. That's the thing about these tests—we don't know they are tests until they're over. To Abraham this is very much the real thing. God is asking him to take his son, and not just his son, his only son—this son Isaac, the son he loves, the son he's waited twenty-five years for, and offer him as a burnt offering.

This might send shivers down our spines, but in those days, child sacrifice was an accepted practice among the surrounding nations. Abraham would have seen this practiced all over the place. But now God is asking it of him.

To make matters worse, Abraham would have had flashbacks all the way back to the first time God talked to him—back in chapter 12. Back then God told him to *go* to a land he would show him. Now God is saying *go* to a mountain I will show you. Back then God was calling him to leave his past and now God is calling him to leave his future.

Here's where we need to be reminded how biblical narratives or stories work. All the stories in the Bible have one hero—that's God. It's his book. The Bible is God showing us who he is, what he's done for us, and how we can respond. So, every story in the Bible is *about* God, but it is *for* us—we're supposed to respond in some way. To repeat, this story is not about Abraham. The moral of this story is not "Be a dad like Isaac had," nor is it that just like Isaac carried the wood on his back, we should all bear the cross.

These stories teach us about God by getting us to join right into this story and identify with some character in the story. The way this story is told—and it is told very well—most of us are to identify with Abraham here. And we're supposed to discover something about God in the process.

Right after this difficult command from God, we might be wondering what he's going to do; the text tells us—with quite a bit of detail. Verse 3: "So Abraham rose early in the morning, saddled his donkey, and took two of his young men with him, and his son Isaac. And he cut wood for the burnt offering and arose and went to the place of which God has told him." That's quite a bit of detail. Whenever we see lots of detail in a story and the plot slows down to do this, we need to pay attention. It looks like Abraham is actually going to go through with this. He's making meticulous preparations to do what God told him to do. You'll also notice it doesn't mention that he woke up Sarah before he left. What's he going to say to her?

The three-day journey gets no attention until they get within eyeshot of the mountain and then the story slows down again. Look at verses 5–8:

> Then Abraham said to his young men, "Stay here with the donkey; I and the boy will go over there and worship and come again to you." [Wait a minute—why does Abraham say that to these two young guys? Is he lying to them? Or maybe he's not going through with it after all. You see the jury is still out and we wonder what Abraham is going to do. This is just to build tension in the story—to keep us guessing.] And Abraham took the wood of the burnt offering and laid it on Isaac his son. And he took in his hand the fire and the knife. And they went, both of them together. And Isaac said to his father Abraham, "My father!" And he said, "Here am I, my son." [Where have we heard those words "here am I" before?] He said, "Behold, the fire and the wood, but where is the lamb for a burnt offering?" Abraham said, "God will provide for himself the lamb for a burnt offering, my son." [Another teaser to build tension. We don't know what is going on inside of Abraham's head right now. Is he really trusting God to provide or is he just trying to sweet talk his son into playing along? Right now, the tension is building until we're on the edge of our seats.] So, they went, both of them together [He just said that a few lines ago—the tension is still building.]

Every story builds to a climax—this is the make or break part of the story when the tension is at its highest. The climax of this story is in verses 9–10: "When they came to the place of which God had told him, Abraham built the altar there and laid the wood in order and bound Isaac his son and laid him on the altar, on top of the wood. Then Abraham reached out his hand and took the knife to slaughter his son." The story has been building to this point, and here we are with Abraham, hand raised with a knife to kill the son of promise. There's our answer—Abraham is going to do it. Unbelievable! It's like the scene from *Psycho* at the Bates Motel when you can see the silhouette of the raised knife on the other side of the shower curtain. We're expecting the worst. Surely not!

Verses 11–12: "But the angel of the LORD called to him from heaven and said, 'Abraham, Abraham!' And he said, [Guess what?] 'Here am I.' He said, 'Do not lay your hand on the boy or do anything to him, for now I

"Why Did God Test Abraham?"

know that you fear God, seeing that you have not withheld your son, your only son, from me.'" Whew!

God does provide a ram for the burnt offering, just like we were all hoping. Notice what Abraham says in verse 14 because this is what the whole story is trying to say: "So Abraham called the name of the place, 'The Lord will provide' [Yahweh Yireh or Jehovah Jireh]; as it is said to this day, 'On the mount of the LORD it shall be provided.'"

That is what this story teaches us about God—Yahweh is the God who provides. He doesn't test us so that we will fail, but so we will be able to experience his provision for us.

Look at the blessing found in verses 17–18: "I will surely bless you, and I will surely multiply your offspring as the stars of heaven and as the sand is on the seashore. And your offspring shall possess the gate of his enemies, and in your offspring shall all the nations of the earth be blessed, because you have obeyed my voice." The promise God made to Abraham way back in chapter 12 is repeated and expanded. God does not test us because he wants us to go our own way and work it out ourselves. He wants us to trust him and obey him, so we can see his hand of provision at work. This can play itself out in a hundred different ways. We can be up against a relational struggle, a difficulty with a stubborn addiction, or a financial crunch of some kind. We all have our issues. We all have our own tests.

God has not changed—he still is the God who provides. That's who he is. The only question that remains is our response to those times of testing in our own lives. Will it be DIY or will it be "Here am I"?

"Why Did God Choose Jacob Over Esau?"

Genesis 25:19–34, ESV
February 12, 2017

Series Title: "Have You Ever Wondered Why?"

PRAYER FOR ILLUMINATION

LORD, we struggle with our choices every day. There seems to be so many of them and we often choose the wrong thing and that leads to trouble. We are amazed at how you choose. Even though it is far above our heads, we pause to praise you for how your ways are above ours. We praise you for choosing us in Christ Jesus and for bringing us into your faith family. So, may the words of my mouth and the meditations of all our hearts be pleasing in your sight, O LORD, our Rock and our Redeemer. Amen.

SERMON

I'd like to introduce you to Victor Lustig. Victor was born in Austria in 1890. He was a charming young man who spoke several different languages—which was very helpful in his occupation. Victor is famous for being one of the most notorious con men in recent history. Over his lifetime, he sold the Eiffel Tower to scrap metal dealers *twice*; he conned Al Capone (the famous Chicago gangster); he sold fake, counterfeit-money-making machines (fake machines that made fake money—how ironic is that?); and even wrote the Ten Commandments for con men. That is quite the legacy.

    I'd also like to introduce you to Yacob ben Yitzak, another famous con man from another era. We know him better as Jacob, the son of Isaac and the brother of Esau. Moses is doing the same thing for us in these two short stories found in Genesis 25—he is introducing us to Jacob. These stories are like a movie trailer, giving us a sneak peek at the life of this man who is to become Israel, the father of God's chosen people.

Just to make sure we all get this connection, remember how God called Abraham, Jacob's grandfather, out of a pagan lifestyle to be the father of a great nation, even though he was old and had no children at the time? This promise of a great nation didn't go through Ishmael, Abraham's first-born son, but through Isaac, Jacob's father. Now the story has progressed another generation, and this time it is Isaac who is having trouble getting an heir. This is starting to develop into a recurring theme—fathers of a great nation who have no kids. So Isaac gets married to Rebekah when he's forty. (That whole story in the previous chapter is pretty amazing itself, *this* close to Valentine's Day, like it is out of some Nicholas Sparks novel—not that I've ever read one.) But time goes on and Isaac doesn't have an heir—Rebekah is barren (which also seems like a recurring theme in these stories).

So, remember back when this was happening to Abraham and Sarah? They tried to fix it themselves and they ended up with Ishmael. Not good. They had to wait twenty-five years for Isaac to come along. Now here is Isaac faced with the same situation and what does he do? He prays to the Lord for his wife, and God grants the answer to his prayer. That's good, but that's not what Moses is trying to say here. It's not "prayer equals heir" or "pray for your wife and you'll have kids all your life." There's more to the story than that.

Not only does God answer Isaac's prayer, he doubles it. It's like those ads on TV: "Act now and we'll double your offer—just add postage and handling." Rebekah is going to have twins and the extra handling part is giving her trouble. It doesn't take very long to realize this is a problem pregnancy. The text says, "the children struggled together within her" (Gen 25:22). Yeah, I'll say. Literally, it means, "the children smashed themselves inside her." There is a cage match going on in there and Rebekah is the cage.

So again, Rebekah goes to God to ask what's up. And what God says is what this story is about and what the whole life of Jacob is about and what the whole history of the nation of Israel is about. So, it's kind of a big deal.

This is what God says:

"Two nations are in your womb, and two peoples from within you shall be divided; the one shall be stronger than the other, the older shall serve the younger" (Gen 25:23).

So, there it is—even before these two were born, God had chosen the younger over the older—so the one that wins the race down the birth canal loses. Kind of ironic, isn't it? How is that even fair? Later, God says in the book of Malachi: "Yet I have loved Jacob, but Esau I have hated" (Mal 1:2b). Translated that means Jacob is God's guy and Esau is not. But our issue is with the timing of this—this was done before we even get a look at these guys. It seems like a done deal before it even starts. Why would God choose Jacob over Esau before they were even born?

We're left with this question dangling in our minds and then the twins are born. The text says, "The first came out red, all his body like a hairy cloak." He is all red—the color red seems important in this story, so remember that. And he looks like he's wearing a fur coat, so they call him Hairy (Esau). There are special privileges for being the oldest—even if it is by just a few seconds. The firstborn was to receive the birthright (*bekora*), which means he gets double the inheritance of all the other sons, and the blessing (*beraka*), the favor of the father. Can you hear the play on words here? These both, by rights, belonged to Esau. But right behind Esau comes his twin brother, hanging onto Esau's heel, still trying to win the race. They call him Jacob which means "heel-grabber," "cheater," or "con man."

From the day of their birth, we skip ahead in the story to the point where both the boys have grown into men. Esau is a skilled hunter and an outdoorsman—nothing wrong with that. Adam's son Abel was an animal guy and he pleased God. So, there's nothing wrong with being a hunter. Isaac loved Esau and he loved eating wild game, so things look pretty good for Esau. Now the text goes on to say, "Jacob was a quiet man, dwelling in tents" (Gen 25:27b). He was a quiet man—what does that mean? Actually, it is the same word used to describe Job and it means "blameless." How could that be? This drives every commentator around the bend. How could someone named "cheater" be blameless? So, they call him "quiet." The truth of the matter is that we know God has chosen Jacob, but we don't know why—yet. We're still wondering about poor old Esau. There is nothing about having a two o'clock shadow and a good shot that should disqualify you. So, what's the deal?

We hope the next episode will help us out—but if we're honest, it only makes it worse. Esau is out in the field because he is an outdoor guy, and Jacob is in his tents making some stew because he is an "in-tents" guy.

For the first time we see the real Esau. And quite frankly, he's a bit of a dolt. He is ruled by his stomach and not his head. He comes in from the field and is so hungry that he thinks he's going to die—really? He eyes this red stew (notice "red" again) and he wants it. We also know good old Hairy has another name: Edom (which also means "red")—Esau will be the father of the Edomites who turn out to be lifelong enemies of the Israelites. So, all of a sudden, Esau (or Hairy or Big Red) wants this stew more than life itself. This sets up what I call the great red stew sting.

We also see Jacob, whose name means cheater or con man, living up to his name. Esau is the mark and a rather gullible one at that. Jacob sees this from a mile away and even we can tell this will be no contest. Here you have a smooth con man pitted against the village idiot—you have Victor Lustig against Larry the Cable Guy. It's pathetic, really.

When he gets the chance, Jacob puts the screws to his own brother to cheat him out of the birthright that belongs to the firstborn. He is heartless and calculating. He makes Esau swear, so he won't back out of it, and he walks away with what belongs to Esau. The perfect scam.

The weird thing is that Esau is none the wiser. He has no clue what has just happened. The text says, "And he ate and drank and rose and went his way" (Gen 25:34). Boom, boom, boom. He doesn't think twice or even once about it. He gets his meal and that's all he wants.

OK, so we can see why Esau doesn't make a good choice. He is impulsive, ruled by his urges. He's none too bright and doesn't value what he should value. The text sums it up by saying "Thus Esau despised his birthright" (Gen 25:34). He ends up marrying pagan wives and is a major disappointment. The Edomites, his nation, refuse to let Israel pass through their land on the way to the promised land, and when Babylon sacks Jerusalem and the temple, the Edomites give the Babylonians a hand. So, we can see why Esau doesn't qualify—but the part that's hard to grasp is why Jacob does qualify.

Jacob is deceptive and self-centered and heartless, always looking out for himself—the consummate con man. He's always in some struggle with someone trying to get ahead. It starts before he's born—fighting with his wombmate. Then he cons Esau out of his birthright. In chapter 27 Jacob goes for round two and rips off Esau's blessing from their father Isaac. Then he ends up matching wits with his father-in-law Laban, who is almost a match for him. After he rips off Laban, he gets into an argument with his wife Rachel over her not being able to have children. He fights with his own children and even fights with God. Is this the guy God has chosen? Yes, this is the guy God has chosen to be father of his special people, Israel.

At this point, you're probably saying, "I don't get it." Guess what? Me neither. Who would you choose if it was between the village idiot and a shyster? I wouldn't pick either one, but God picks Jacob. Does he look like he's worthy? That, actually, is the point: he's not.

Here's where the apostle Paul comes to our rescue. This is what he says to the Roman Christians:

> And not only so, but also when Rebekah had conceived children by one man, our forefather Isaac, though they were not yet born and had done nothing either good or bad—in order that God's purpose of election might continue, not because of works but because of him who calls—she was told, "the older will serve the younger" as it is written, "Jacob I loved, but Esau I hated . . . " So, then it depends not on human will or exertion, but on God who has mercy. (Rom 9:10-13, 16)

So in the end, God chooses Jacob over Esau—not because one was more deserving than the other, but because neither was worthy. He chose one, so he might bless many. That's why he chose Abraham, that's why he chose Isaac, that's why he chose Jacob, and strange as it seems, that is why he has chosen us—so that we might bless many others. We are his—not because of what we have done or that we are nicer than other people who won't be going anywhere near a church service this morning. We are his due to God's gracious choosing—nothing more, nothing less, nothing else. The hardest part for us is just to get our heads around it.

This is not about a theological question to debate—as much as we like to debate that sort of thing around here. This is about a God who chooses each one of us to be a blessing to those around us and those beyond us. We are chosen to be a blessing to others.

The question that remains today is not, "Why did God choose Jacob over Esau?," it is, "Who has God called me to bless today?" I would wager a guess he has already put someone on your mind. Don't waste your time asking, "Why me?," when you could be asking, "Who can I choose to bless today?" *That's* the question—and that's no con.

"Take This Job and Love It"

Isaiah 6:1–13, ESV
March 8, 2015, Lent III

Series Title: "The Fifth Gospel: Isaiah's Message for Us"

PRAYER FOR ILLUMINATION

LORD, we come here today because you have called us—you've called us to be your children, to be a family that loves and cares for each other, you've called us to be right here worshipping you this morning, and you've called each of us to serve you in a unique way. You know a lot more about this calling than we do—to us it can seem pretty mysterious. So, speak to us plainly about how we might obey your calling of each and all of us. And may the words of my mouth and meditations of all our hearts be pleasing in your sight, O LORD our Rock and our Redeemer. Amen

SERMON

All of us have been asked at one time or another, "What do you want to be when you grow up?" You might have said, "A doctor, a nurse, a cowboy, a millionaire, a rock star, an astronaut, a professional athlete, a teacher." You probably didn't say, "A telemarketer, a used car salesman, a politician, or a TV weatherman." Why? Because some jobs seem more attractive than others. Other jobs don't appeal to us because they have bad reputations. Some of us may find ourselves doing something we never intended to do. Being a pastor was not on my radar as a kid. At one time or another we all struggle with this whole idea of our calling. All of us have days when we wonder if we are where we're supposed to be.

Mark Buchanan, a pastor-turned-professor has this advice for us:

> When you have had one of those take-this-job-and-shove-it-days, try this. On your way home, stop at your pharmacy and go to the section where they have thermometers. You will need to purchase a rectal thermometer made by the Q-tip Company. Be sure that you get this brand. When you get home, lock your doors, draw the drapes, and disconnect the phone so you will not be disturbed during your therapy. Change into something comfortable, such as a sweat suit, and lie down on your bed. Open the package containing the thermometer, remove it, and carefully place it on the bedside table so that it will not become chipped or broken. Take the written material that accompanies the thermometer. As you read, notice in small print this statement: "Every rectal thermometer made by Q-tip is *personally* tested." Close your eyes. Say out loud five times, "Thank you, oh thank you, that I do not work in quality control at the Q-tip Company."

Maybe now we have a better understanding of what it means to be a prophet. No one wants to be a prophet, not even prophets—especially prophets. To be a prophet is a life sentence for being an outsider, a crazy wacko who hears voices, a God whisperer. If people like you, that usually means you aren't doing your job—you are a false prophet. If you do your job properly, people usually hate your guts. You can't win for losing. You are one of those strange people who live in what the Celts called the thin places, where the boundaries between heaven and earth were the thinnest. This is a tough job. That's why most prophets have to be recruited—hard! Very few are just waiting to sign up. That's why we're starting six chapters into Isaiah instead of at chapter 1. It's here where Isaiah tells us how he was called.

Calling stories are especially important for prophets because they can point back to these experiences and say, "See, it wasn't my idea. It was God's. I'm not doing and saying all this stuff because I want to, but because he told me to." We start with Isaiah's call because then we can understand what he says and does. We start with Isaiah's call, so we might get fresh insight into our own calling—no matter what that calling might be. How has God called me? In Isaiah's call story we might find meaning for our own call stories.

Isaiah's career as a prophet begins in about 740 BC. King Uzziah has just died and the southern nation of Judah is in a bit of a tizzy. To the Northeast, the aggressive and brutal Assyrians are starting to salivate over

"Take This Job and Love It"

this little land bridge called Israel. They are led by their bloodthirsty king Tiglath-pileser III. (You football fans have probably heard of RG3—well, this is TP3.) This is a time of national crisis. God's people are far from faithful to their covenant with Yahweh, and God wants someone to be his mouthpiece in these tumultuous times. He chooses Isaiah.

Call stories have at least three things in common: a caller (the one who does the calling), the "callee" (the one who receives the call), and the call itself (the actual commissioning).

We start with the caller because that's where Isaiah starts in verses 1–4. Maybe you've been to an IMAX theatre or one of those attractions at Disneyland or Disney World where you are in the middle of a room with special effects all over the place and you feel like you're right in the middle of the action. You are terrified, exhilarated, and nauseous all at the same time. Take that, multiply it by a thousand, and you get close to what happens here. God shows up in a dramatic way in the temple and all heaven breaks loose. Yes, King Uzziah has died, and everyone back then was nervous whenever a king died. The whole country seemed vulnerable to attacks from neighboring nations until a new king was crowned. But here is the real King. Notice how God is described in royal terms here: he's sitting on a throne; he is high and lifted up; he is majestic and transcendent. And just the train or hem of his royal robe is enough to fill the entire temple. He is served by the seraphim—the burning ones—and they call out to each other to announce the presence of this King among kings, "Holy, holy, holy is the LORD of Hosts; the whole earth is full of his glory!" (Isa 6:3). The Hebrew language doesn't have a word for "holiest," so normally they just repeat the word. But here, and only here, is it repeated twice: holy, holy, holy—this One is the holiest, he is perfectly and infinitely holy. We don't hear these words again until John sees God in heaven in the book of Revelation. God is holy which means he is completely different from us—he is completely good and pure and powerful. The whole earth is full of his glory. This glory is his consuming brightness that shines from his holiness. His holiness and his glory are inseparable. One commentator says, "Glory is God's all-present holiness."[1]

And the voice of this King makes the foundations of the temple tremble and he is surrounded by thick smoke. This is the One who calls. Do you think he has Isaiah's attention? Maybe the more important question is, "Does he have our attention?" This is the same God who calls

---

1. Motyer, *Prophecy of Isaiah*, 77.

each and all of us. Sometimes we have trouble understanding our calling. Could it be we haven't understood who it is who has called us? Have we lost sight of the complete holiness and majesty of God? Have we somehow duped ourselves into thinking it's really more about me than it is about the one who calls me? How we respond to his calling is often how we respond to worship. Do we leave a worship service and say, "I really liked worship today. It really spoke to me." What we really mean is: I'm there to be served, or I'm there because all my friends are there. Isaiah starts with the caller because he's the one that makes this whole thing work.

But the caller is there to call the "callee" as we see in verse 5. Isaiah isn't sitting there yawning, saying, "All these pyrotechnics are fine, but they didn't really speak to me." When you are face to face with that kind of brilliant holiness, you can't help but see your own utter unworthiness. We can go along for ages without coming to grips with our own sinfulness until we catch a glimpse of true holiness. Then we fall apart. When I was in PEI we used to have a conference every year at the Confederation Centre of the Arts. I got to be the worship leader and so they gave me my own green room complete with a theatrical makeup mirror. This is a huge mirror surrounded with powerful lights so that you can see everything, I mean everything—every imperfection, every blemish, everything. I saw imperfections on my imperfections. I saw that I didn't have hair in the places I should have, and I had hair in places I shouldn't. We see all this in light of the way it should be. This is Isaiah's experience. He knows he is one, who by comparison, is filthy compared to the purity of God's holiness. And he realizes that everyone else is in the same boat. He is utterly lost, and he fears for his life. But then we get a picture of God's holy love in verses 6–7. God brings forgiveness so that we stand forgiven before him—no longer lost but found, no longer dead in our sins but alive to God through his grace.

This is the role of us, the "callee"—not to sit in judgment over the caller but to respond in humble obedience to him, to receive his gracious forgiveness, and to open our hearts and lives to his calling.

So now we get to the calling itself in verse 8. A lot of sermons end with verse 8. And when they do, this text sound an awful lot like a call to worship—the majesty of God and the repentant worshipper who wants to be picked to go and speak for God. It would be nice just to stop with verse 8, but since Isaiah doesn't. Read verses 9–13. It turns out that this text is not a call to worship but a call to service—but these two might be closer than we think.

And he said, "Go, and say to this people:

'Keep on hearing, but do not understand;
keep on seeing, but do not perceive.'
Make the heart of this people dull,
    and their ears heavy,
    and blind their eyes;
lest they see with their eyes,
    and hear with their ears,
and understand with their hearts,
    and turn and be healed."
Then I said, "How long, O Lord?"
And he said:
"Until cities lie waste
    without inhabitant,
and houses without people,
    and the land is a desolate waste,
and the Lord removes people far away,
    and the forsaken places are many in the midst of the land.
And though a tenth remain in it,
    it will be burned again,
like a terebinth or an oak,
    whose stump remains."

It's a serious understatement to say that sometimes God's calling doesn't make much sense to us. Why would God call Isaiah to do a job that would only make his people more hardened and resistant to God's call to repent? We don't get it because we have started here in chapter 6 instead of with chapter 1. Chapters 1–5 of Isaiah explain what God means here in chapter 6. We get a picture of just how hard-boiled God's people have become.

They have ears, but they aren't willing to hear. They have eyes but will not see. Their hearts are dull and hardened to the truth. Isaiah is called to a task where he will not succeed. That bothers us—imagine what Isaiah is feeling now. It's true that once we reach a certain point, we just seem to get worse, and hearing the truth only makes us madder, not better. The same holds true today. Every time we come here to worship we do not leave the same way. Either our hearts have been softened toward God or they have been hardened. A brittle heart is a little heart and soon we can't feel at all.

No wonder Isaiah asks, "How long, O Lord?" When will this end? We don't like God's answer any more than what he just said. This is to last until the land is decimated and God's people are carted off into captivity. Then with only a fraction left, it will be decimated again like trees chopped down to bare stumps. That's a pretty bleak picture unless we catch the hint right at the end of verse 13. "The holy seed is its stump." In other words, the land may be chopped down like trees, but God will still salvage the stump which will be the basis of a new forest—a remnant of people who will still enjoy fellowship with God, a remnant from which will come—eventually—the one who will make all things new. Even though much of this feels like bad news, with Isaiah and the rest of the prophets, bad news is never the final word. God is always at work bringing good news out of the bad, bringing his salvation out of judgment, saving his faithful ones out of those who refuse to believe and repent.

So, we know that calling starts with the caller. It does with Isaiah and it does with us. This requires a whole shift in how we look at our calling in life. We tend to look first at ourselves as the "callees." We want to be worthy of our calling. We want to earn the right to be given a calling. But Isaiah just stands there, completely unworthy, with lips swollen and blistered from the cleansing red hot coal and mumbles, "Here am I, send me" (Isa 6:8b). Our calling isn't about us at all.

Sometimes we think our calling is about what we accomplish. I want a calling that leaves behind a great legacy, lots of accomplishments, and a lot that would make everyone look at with awe and respect. Isaiah reminds us it's not about us or our accomplishments. It's about faithfulness to the end—no matter what happens in the meantime.

It all boils down to this: our calling is about the Caller—this thrice holy One. He is the One who calls us, who shows us how we can live lives that honor him through our faithfulness. What we do with our calling is what we offer back to the Caller as a sacrifice of praise. And we know we have learned this lesson when we can't tell the difference between a call to service and a call to worship. Because with God, our work is worship.

"The Jesus Cruise"

Mark 4:35-41, ESV
April 1, 2012, Palm Sunday

Series Title: "Mark: Keeping Up with the King"

PRAYER FOR ILLUMINATION

LORD you know we are often afraid, and our faith vanishes like the wind. Help us trust in you no matter what happens so we can experience your sweet presence. So, may the words of my mouth and the meditations of all our hearts be pleasing in your sight, O LORD our Rock and our Redeemer. Amen.

SERMON

All of us have one of these—no matter how old we are or how tough we think we are. We all have something that that scares us to death—that paralyzes us with fear. I remember having all kinds of fears when I was growing up. But my parents had named me "Blayne" which means "yellow," so what chance did I have? I remember being afraid of snakes and lightning storms and heights and people. But the worst was water. Water really scared me. It was so dangerous. I wouldn't take swimming lessons because that meant I had to go in the water.

When I took a bath, I only put in about three inches of water because I didn't want to drown. So, where you do think God would call someone so afraid of water to be a pastor? On an island. After fourteen years on Prince Edward Island, I thought I had my fear of water conquered. Then five summers ago we went back. I felt so confident that one day at noon I decided to take a canoe out in the ocean for a quick paddle. I've told you this story before, so I'll be brief. The wind and the tide conspired against me and it wasn't long before I was five kilometers off shore surrounded by high ocean waves. All of a sudden, I remembered why I was afraid of water. Long story short, I flagged down a small yacht and they pried my hands from the sides of the canoe and took me on board. They were all a bit drunk, but it didn't matter. I was saved from the water.

That day I caught a whiff of what might have been going through the minds of the disciples that night on the Sea of Galilee. It's mighty hard for me to read this passage and not be preoccupied with how these twelve guys must have been feeling when they were facing what looked like an imperfect death in the perfect storm. I think that's perfectly normal.

When we look at this story we see the disciples and their fear. We see the disciples caught in a terrifying experience, and they call out to Jesus to deliver them from the storm. And he does—hallelujah! You know we all have storms in our lives and even though Jesus never promises smooth sailing, he'll be there to see us through the toughest storm.

And we all have storms—sometimes big ones. In the words of the great philosopher Amanda Marshall: "Everybody's got a story that could break your heart."

We are tempted to think this way because we assume this story is about the disciples and then, by extension, about us. But is that true? Is Mark telling us this story to tell us something about the disciples? If this story is not about the disciples, then who is it about? You can use your Sunday school answer here. It's about Jesus.

Mark has just given us a short timeout by recording some of Jesus' teaching and now he's back to showing us all these miracles Jesus is performing. This story is the first of four miracle stories in a row.

So, it turns out this story has a hero and it's not the disciples. As a matter of fact, this is where Mark starts showing us Jesus' disciples for who they really are. Up to this point, we get the impression that lots of other people are on the outside and the disciples are on the inside, so they must be really brilliant, right? Wrong! As Mark tells the story of Jesus, we start to think that when Jesus chose the twelve disciples, he must have been grading on a curve. These guys don't look very bright. And today's story is just the beginning.

Does that bother you? That these followers of Jesus were dense and out of it a lot of the time? Even though Jesus spent extra time explaining

"The Jesus Cruise"

everything to them, they often were favored failures. I don't find that discouraging. I find that encouraging—don't you? It gives me more hope.

So, this story isn't about these dumb disciples going through a storm. It's about Jesus. Mark is still answering the same question—who is this Jesus? This story gives us some insight into that question. He connects this story with the other stories in chapter 4.

"On that day, when evening had come"—Mark is making a connection between Jesus' teaching and his actions. He says to his disciples after a full day of teaching the huge crowds, "Let's go over to the other side of the lake" (Mark 4:35). It's only an eight kilometer trip to the other side of the Sea of Galilee—no big deal, if the winds didn't get up.

I don't know about you, but all of a sudden, this tune comes to my mind: [Sing to the tune of the theme to *Gilligan's Island*.]

> Just sit right back and you'll hear a tale,
> A tale of a fateful trip
> That started from this ancient port
> Aboard this tiny ship.
>
> The mate was a mighty sailing man,
> The Savior brave and sure.
> Twelve passengers set sail that day
> For a three-hour tour, a three-hour tour.
>
> The weather started getting rough,
> The tiny ship was tossed
> If not for the presence of their sleeping Lord
> Their lunches would be lost; their lunches would be lost . . .

You get what I mean.

Part way through the trip, the winds get up and the waves are spilling over the edge of the boat. It's serious. Even the four fishermen are freaking out. Do you know why? Because the disciples are afraid of water too. Actually, all the Jews were. Water to them was a symbol of evil and chaos. If it wasn't for that giving up bacon thing, I could probably be Jewish.

The whole situation is chaotic, everyone is losing it. Everyone but Jesus who is catching a power nap in the back of the boat. What a contrast!

The disciples don't get it. They think Jesus is asleep because he doesn't care, but that's not it. Jesus is asleep because he's tired and, apparently, he's not afraid of water.

Notice what they call him—"Teacher." When it's all on the line, the truth comes out—not "Lord" or "Master," just "Teacher." That's like going up to the Prime Minister and saying, "Hey, dude."

Jesus gets up and barks orders to the wind and the waves—"Peace, be still!"—and immediately, in the words of the Message, "the wind ran out of breath and the sea became smooth as glass" (Mark 4:39). Everything was quiet—too quiet. The disciples see what happened and now they are really scared.

Mark says literally, "They feared a great fear." They realized they were in the same boat with a guy who had the authority to change the weather, and they had just looked like a bunch of complete idiots right in front of him. They stammer with their jaws hitting the bottom of the boat, "Who then is this, that even the wind and the sea obey him?" (Mark 4:41). Even the disciples know this story isn't about them, it's about Jesus—this one who has this kind of authority.

It's not about us going through storms, it's about Jesus being able to calm storms. He is in control.

But before we're through, maybe we should pay closer attention to what this powerful Jesus says to his fraidy-cat disciples. He says, "Why are you so afraid? Have you still no faith?" (Mark 4:40).

In other words, he expects his followers to trust him. The disciples' fear was a sign they hadn't grown to trust him enough yet. They were overlooking the necessary and asking for the unnecessary. They were asking for deliverance and Jesus was asking them to trust him.

So, what is Mark saying? He's saying this story is *about* Jesus. But this story is *for* us.

It's for us because this One who can calm the seas wants us to trust him and not be afraid. He has it all under control—even when we fear for our lives.

So, when we fear that we'll be alone—Jesus says, "Trust me. I've got it under control."

When we fear that we'll be a failure—Jesus says, "Trust me. I've got it all under control."

When we fear what others think of us—Jesus says, "Trust me. I've got it all under control."

When we fear where the next month's rent will come from—Jesus says, "Trust me. I've got it all under control."

"The Jesus Cruise"

When the weight of final assignments and upcoming exams has us coming unglued—Jesus says, "Trust me. I've got it all in control."

When life is rough, and we are tempted to be paralyzed by our fears, Jesus says to us, "Don't look at the waves, look at me. Trust me. I've got it all under control."

He says, "I am with you always, even to the end of the age" (Matt 28:20). Get to know me, talk to me, trust me, spend time with me, sit down and eat with me. When we do, we realize how stupid it is to try to control everything that happens to us. Jesus had to use a storm that made seasoned fishermen scream like little girls to teach his disciples that he is in control. He used three foot waves in the middle of Northumberland Strait to teach me the same lesson. I have higher hopes for you.

"An Heir-Raising Adventure"

Luke 7:11–17, ESV
October 13, 2013

Series Title: "What on Earth is God Up To?"

PRAYER FOR ILLUMINATION

LORD, sometimes our heads get in the way of our hearts and we can think and reason our way out of what we know we should be feeling toward those whom you love. Help us to love as you love. May the things that break your heart also break ours. And may the words of my mouth and the meditations of all our hearts be pleasing in your sight, O LORD, our Rock and our Redeemer. Amen.

SERMON

Some combinations feel like they were made for each other, like peanut butter and jam, love and marriage, a horse and carriage, Batman and Robin, yin and yang, Will and Kate, Simon and Garfunkel, Jack and Jill, Dumb and Dumber, Bert and Ernie, fish and chips, Pinky and the Brain. But then there are some rather unlikely combinations. Like our dog back on the farm. She was a cross between a Beagle and a Chihuahua. Her name was Fifi. What do you call a cross between a Beagle and a Chihuahua? You call it a "Bowowa." There are other rather bizarre combinations. Like what do you get when you cross a parrot and a centipede? A walkie talkie. Or what do you get when you cross a cheetah and a hamburger? Fast food. Or what do you get when you cross a dog and a daisy? A Collie flower. Or what do you get if you cross a galaxy with a toad? Star Warts. Or even better, what do you get

"An Heir-Raising Adventure"

when you combine Jesus and an excited crowd of his disciples with a crowd heading to the cemetery? You get an heir-raising adventure. And this is where Luke brings us this morning.

We see Jesus and his entourage heading into town while this other entourage is heading out. One crowd is filled with excitement and anticipation; the other is marked by grief and shrill wailing. It's important that we know why Luke is telling us this story right at this time. This is one of seven miracles that Luke records that no other Gospel writer does; that, in itself, should cause us to wonder. We see that he has finished preaching what we call his Sermon on the Plain—part of which we listened to last week—and then he has just healed the centurion's servant who was near death. Now he is making his way south—about ten kilometers southeast of his hometown of Nazareth—to a town called Nain. There is something we've learned about the way Luke is telling the story of Jesus. Right from the get-go he told us he would be giving us an orderly account of Jesus' life. So, we're on the lookout for this in Luke's story.

Maybe you've noticed, but in Luke's Gospel he often tells a story about some guy getting healed by Jesus and then the next story is about him ministering to a girl. So, Jesus has just healed the servant of a centurion, and we've been tipped off that maybe this time he'll be helping a woman. But we're surprised to see that it is a guy who has died and is being taken by a considerable crowd out to the cemetery. It's not any guy—it's the only son of a widow—and he has a real problem—he's not breathing anymore. Jesus has done amazing things already, but raising the dead? Really? Who could do that? Well Elijah could—back in 1 Kings 17—but he was a great prophet. All this is running through our minds and Luke definitely has our attention. What is he going to do?

True to form, this is where Jesus surprises us yet again. Just when we think he's going to zig, he zags. We find out firsthand that this story isn't really about this deceased young man—it's about how Jesus deals with his widowed mother.

It's all very strange. Here we have two big crowds with all kinds of noise going on and all of a sudden all the noise fades into the background—crowds, wailing, disciples, everything—and all we see is Jesus and this widow. Luke tells us she's a widow (which means her only son was her last means of support—she is destined to a life of abject poverty). There is a considerable crowd with *her*, Jesus saw *her*, had compassion on *her*, and spoke to *her*.

We see some things that we might have expected. Jesus is pushing the envelope a bit by touching the stretcher they were carrying to the cemetery. That should have made him ritually unclean for a week. But Jesus isn't about letting unclean things defile him; he is there to make defiled things clean.

We see Jesus acting in power. We can see that because Luke doesn't want us to miss it. He goes out of his way to show how this episode echoes the story of Elijah raising the widow's son back in 1 Kings 17—there are too many parallels between these stories to be an accident. But Jesus is shown to trump Elijah. To raise this young man, Jesus doesn't throw himself on top of the corpse like Elijah did. Imagine the scene that would have caused. He simply spoke the words and it was so.

So, what is it about this story that is most memorable? It's verse 13. This is the climax of the entire story: "And when the Lord saw her, he had compassion on her and said to her, 'Do not weep.'" He had compassion on her. What does that mean? The word here actually refers to people's intestines, their bowels, their viscera. There are all kinds of temptation here to use some bathroom humor here, but we won't (besides we've already made reference to a funeral "bier," and I resisted that too). This is too important. When Jesus sees this woman, his response is to have his guts churn inside of him—with a depth of feeling that cannot be put into words—only action. Jesus is moved with compassion for her and her plight. What is not center stage here is Jesus' power, even though there is plenty of it—and it's greater than even Elijah's. What is most evident about Jesus here is his compassion.

What does he say to this woman—this woman who has nowhere else to go, who will be the poorest of the poor, alone and destitute, who has more reason to cry her eyes out than anyone else? He says to her, "Do not weep." If we have any counselors in the crowd this morning, you are probably scratching your heads right about now. Why does Jesus tell her not to weep? Of course, she should be weeping—loudly. She needs to get it all out, to grieve and not hold back. Doesn't Jesus know that telling her not to weep is just plain bad counselling practice? So much for "wonderful counselor."

But what Jesus is saying here is not bad counselling technique—it is the gospel, the gospel of the kingdom. Remember last week we heard Jesus say, "Blessed are you who weep now, for you shall be comforted" and "Woe to you who laugh now, for you shall mourn and weep" (Luke 6:21b, 25b). Jesus is just practicing what he's preaching. He comes announcing God's kingdom and the salvation that comes through it. Part of that salvation is that tears will be wiped away in the shadow of the cross and the empty

"An Heir-Raising Adventure"

tomb, and we are freed to experience outrageous joy—the joy of belonging to God and being part of his kingdom. This is not a lesson on grief counselling—it's a lesson on the gospel.

And as we have chance to look back at this story we begin to see what it is about. Here, Jesus reminds us that compassion is *real* power. That's it. Compassion is *real* power. This upside down kingdom shows us that treating others with compassion in the name of this Jesus can be one of the most powerful things we can do. We probably already know that, but maybe we've forgotten it this morning. Compassion takes real guts.

Phil Callaway tells this true story of two teenage girls, Kaitlyn and Amy, who worked at their local grocery store. One of their fellow workers was Tara, a single mother of four. Tara worked very hard just to make ends meet, but one day her fourteen-year-old son Daniel took her old van for a joyride. He collided with a truck and was killed. Tara's already difficult life was in shambles. Kaitlyn and Amy saw what was happening and decided to do something about it. They talked their boss into giving them five hundred dollars to secure the best venue in town to have a benefit concert for Tara. They went around to all the businesses in town asking for donations of auction items—only one business refused. Country artist Paul Brandt gave them an autographed guitar. Kaitlyn's dad Gord was an accomplished guitarist who started asking friends to come for this special occasion and they showed up from all over. Kaitlyn and her mom Liz told Tara about all this, and Tara was blown away.

"I don't have anything to wear," she said.

Kaitlyn and her mom took her shopping. Tara found out about they were believers and said, "I don't even have a Bible."

They got her one.

Hundreds of people met on a Sunday evening and plenty enough money was raised to help Tara with her expenses. The local Dodge dealer handed her the keys to a van.

Tara had all kinds of questions—like "Why did this have to happen?" But also, "Why would people act this way to me?" She opened the Bible Kaitlyn and her mom gave her and she found her answer. She phoned a local pastor and said, "I need to talk to a minister—right now!"

Pastor Jason was able to lead her to Christ that night.

Not every story ends this way. Sometimes people refuse our compassion—they killed Jesus for his. On this occasion, the crowd was extremely impressed and amazed. They gave him the greatest compliment they could think of at the time—Jesus is a great prophet—even greater than Elijah. In Jesus, God's favor is pouring out on his people. Their tune will change in time, and the crowds will be calling for his death. So, there is no one-to-one correspondence between our compassion and people's response—but that doesn't change the truth of the matter. Compassion is *real* power. It is the power of the kingdom. And thanks to Jesus, we all have the guts to do it.

That brings us to our three life-changing questions: *What on earth has gone wrong?* Part of what has gone wrong is we often live like everyone else. We live for ourselves, for the power plays that rank us ahead of others rather than caring for them as their servants. We may have lost the power that comes from true gospel compassion.

What on earth is God up to? God is building his kingdom through all his children who realize the way up is to go down, the way ahead is to be willing to stand behind, and the way to power is to give it away in acts of compassion.

How on earth can we be the church in this new space? By listening to Jesus and following his lead. By remembering that compassion is *real* power—that our lives aren't measured by what we *make* of ourselves but by how we *give* of ourselves for the sake of others in Jesus' name.

"Lost and Found"

Luke 15:1–32, ESV
March 2, 2014

Series Title: "What on Earth is God Up To?"

PRAYER FOR ILLUMINATION

LORD, forgive us those times when we were celebrating when we should have been mourning, the times when we have been sour and self-righteous instead of repenting, and the times we have been mourning when we should have been celebrating. And may the words of my mouth and the meditations of all our hearts be pleasing in your sight, O LORD our Rock and our Redeemer. Amen.

SERMON

Sometimes we celebrate the dumbest things. If you looked this up on a calendar, you would know that yesterday was National Pig Day (on the Sabbath!). If you have any Jewish friends, chances are they were very confused yesterday. Today is officially Old Stuff Day which is why I'm preaching today instead of Pastor Kevin. Tomorrow is If Pets Had Thumbs Day. (I'm not kidding—look it up.) March 5 is Multiple Personality Day (so is March 6 and 7). March 14 is National Potato Chip Day. And the next day is the Ides of March—I'm sure there's no connection.

Last week we celebrated Olympic Gold in men's hockey. Last fall we celebrated the big Grey Cup win. Next week we'll be celebrating National Volleyball Men's Gold. (No pressure, guys.)

There have been some more substantial celebrations as well. The last few months we have been celebrating a whole lot of births around here (a glowing testament to last year's long winter). We celebrate birthdays, anniversaries, graduations—a lot of good things. We might even say: we are what we celebrate. And that is what brings us to Luke 15.

This is one of the most well-known passages in all the Bible. The problem with that is that we all think we know what it means. So did I. I was ready to roll on Friday and then I watched a video clip by Andy Stanley. I had to start all over. Can I confess something to you? Andy Stanley bugs me. Every time I read him or listen to him, he messes me up and I'm left marveling at God's astounding grace.

I went back and looked at Luke 15 again, and I saw something I hadn't seen before. It's all about celebrating. It starts with a celebration and ends with one, and there are celebrations all the way through it.

Luke 15 opens with Jesus throwing a party for tax collectors and sinners—those who were definitely on the outside of what was spiritually respectable. Those whose lives were far from spotless and were caught up in a cycle of sinfulness and self-loathing. Then the Pharisees and scribes show up. This is a change of strategy for them. Up to this point, they have been inviting Jesus to their parties, and he's always made them mad. Now, they're going to crash Jesus' party. But, of course, it's from the outside because they wouldn't be caught dead hanging out with that kind of riffraff. They stay outside at a safe distance and growl a collective harrumph because Jesus is partying with pagans. They don't like how Jesus is celebrating.

That is what prompts Jesus to tell these three stories. Usually we just jump ahead to the third one—what we call the parable of the prodigal son. I think that's a mistake—like skipping the first two verses of a song or hymn. We need to hear all Jesus is saying here, and we can't unless we listen to all three.

Jesus starts with a lost lamb. Jesus leads with what everyone knows about sheep. Sheep are dumb. They get lost a lot. They are helpless. They need a shepherd. This shepherd had a hundred of them—that's quite a flock. One got lost. What does the shepherd do? He leaves the ninety-nine in a safe place and goes looking for the lost lamb. When he finds it, he hoists it up on his shoulders and carries it back to the rest of the flock. He's so happy he's found his sheep that he texts all his friends to come over for chicken wings and frog legs—probably not leg of lamb (because that would be counterproductive, wouldn't it?). Then Jesus says, "Just so, I tell you, there

"Lost and Found"

will be more joy in heaven over one sinner who repents than over ninety-nine righteous persons who need no repentance" (Luke 15:7). Notice the simple rhythm of this story? Something gets lost, then it's found, and then there's a celebration. Or, as Eugene Lowery says, "*Lost . . . found . . . party.*"

Then Jesus ups the ante in the next story. This time it's not one sheep out of one hundred but one coin out of ten. This rather poor lady has just lost 10 percent of her life savings. So, she lights a lamp and searches everywhere until she finds the lost loonie. Then she Facebooks all her friends and invites them over for a celebration. Did you see it again? *Lost . . . found . . . party.*

Now we get to the third story—the one we've all been waiting for. We call it the parable of the prodigal son because we think prodigal means rebellious. But we're wrong. Prodigal means extravagant. If anyone in this story is extravagant, it's the father. Jesus reminds us this story is really about God by saying, "There was a *man* who had two sons" (Luke 15:11).

The story begins with the youngest son not acting very "sonly" and the father not acting very fatherly. The youngest son has the gall to ask his father for his share of the inheritance while his father is still alive. In other words, what he's saying to his father is, "I can't wait for you to die" (in both senses of that phrase). The father does the unexpected—he does as his son asks. Back in those days the father had the right of life and death over his children. To cave like this would seem scandalous. But then the younger son adds insult to injury by cashing in his inheritance for a backpack full of gift cards and heads off to a pagan country. There he whoops it up in all kinds of wild living until he's blown the whole thing.

As soon as bankruptcy hits, so does a famine and this guy is on the skids. He's destitute. He's a street person who hires himself out as a day laborer to feed pigs, and even the pigs have more than he does. "And he was longing to be fed with the pods that the pigs ate, but no one gave him anything" (Luke 15:16). One day while he is slopping the hogs, the lights finally come on. Jesus says, "But when he came to himself" (Luke 15:17a). A thought strikes him: "I'm lost." Think about it: when you're a Jewish guy and when you look around, and all you can see are pigs, pods, and pig poop—you're lost! Here we have the first part of our rhythm again: *Lost*. But this time Jesus slows down the story and gives us some details. This time it's not just *lost*, but Jesus takes the time to remind us that the lost are indeed lost.

This guy is lost, and he knows it. He doesn't even try to imagine he'd be received back into the family. The best he's hoping for is to get back on as a hired hand. Being a son again is more than he can imagine. All he knows for sure is that he's lost. The people Jesus is hanging around are lost too. And they know it. They are hopeless and powerless to do anything about their situation. They will need help if they ever will be found.

So, the story continues, and this hollow shell of a son starts to slink home just so he can have a roof over his head and something in his stomach. He left home defiantly, and he comes back home defeated. And here is where the story really picks up speed. Jesus says, "But while he was still a long way off, his father saw him" (Luke 15:20). How could that be? It's because ever since the son left home, the father was looking for him to come back. Then, that one day as the father is sitting in his rocking chair scanning the horizon, he sees a wispy purple figure on a distant hill. This silhouette has a drooping head and slouched shoulders and is staggering a bit under the stare of the hot sun. But the father knows who it is, because he has been waiting for this day for years. Then he does something else that isn't very fatherly. He hitches up his robes and starts running like a crazy person to meet his son. Fathers back then didn't run like that—especially to meet someone who had brought him complete disgrace. But the father was not filled with anger or contempt, but his heart was filled with compassion. So, he warmly embraces his long-lost son and graciously gives him way more than he deserves. He gives him sandals for his feet, the best robe, and a ring for his finger—all signs of sonship. We go from *lost* to *found*. The lost are lost but now the lost are found. It doesn't matter what we're talking about: a lamb, a loonie, or a loser—they were all lost and needed someone to find them. The father runs to his lost son and he is found.

Then the fun part begins: the father says, "Bring the fattened calf and kill it, and let us eat and celebrate. For this my son was dead, and is alive again; he was lost, and is found. And they began to celebrate" (Luke 15:24). *Lost . . . found . . . party*. The lost are lost, the lost are found, and it's party time.

But this time there is someone who is upset with this whole party thing (besides the fattened calf)—it's the older brother. He's out on the back forty when he hears music and dancing and smells barbequed veal. He growls a self-righteous harrumph and won't come in and join the party. Where have we seen this before? Now the father is coming out to find his older son, just like he did with his younger one, and invites him to the party. But the older son also acts like he's not part of the family either. He refers to his brother as "this son of yours" and speaks about "slaving" for his father

"Lost and Found"

all these years, like he's a hired hand (Luke 15:30). But notice that the father is still inviting this son, who in the words of Mark Twain, "is a good man in the worst sense of the word." Through this father's pleading, Jesus isn't just inviting the down-and-out to the party but the ones who already think they're in. Jesus is seeking the older brother types too.

This is good news for me because I'm an older brother—literally. I grew up on a farm and had a younger brother pretty much like this guy in the story. While I tried to do everything right, he seemed to do everything wrong. He turned into an alcoholic; he broke up his marriage and other marriages as well; he treated my dad with contempt and brought the farm to financial ruin. And yet my dad kept speaking of him in the most glowing terms. To be honest, that really drove me crazy. Then in the summer of 2003, my brother was found—he finally came home, and I wasn't there for the party. In early September of that year he was killed in a farming accident—and the message of this story in Luke 15 brought me to my knees. God used this story to remind me that it's not the good people who can join the party—it's those who repent.

This is what God is up to. He wants everyone to be saved—whether they know they need it or not. He is seeking and saving those who are lost so they can join him in a party that will never end. So, in the end, and all the way through, Luke 15 is all about celebrating. In it, Jesus reminds us the lost are lost, the lost can be found, and when the lost are found it's party time. For where your party is, there will your heart be also. Amen.

"Party with a Purpose"

Luke 19:1–10, ESV
April 6, 2014, Lent V

Series Title: "What on Earth is God Up To?"

PRAYER FOR ILLUMINATION

O LORD, forgive us for seeing only ourselves and what we think is important to us. Help us to see how you look at us and for us, so our focus is on you and not on us. And may the words of my mouth and the meditations of all our hearts be pleasing in your sight, O LORD, our Rock and our Redeemer. Amen.

SERMON

Our world has never been an easy place for short people, the vertically challenged. Ask Napoleon, Rumpelstiltskin, or Danny DeVito. It's hard to gain respect when people are making fun of you. The truth is, we all have issues, and some of these are easier to hide than others. Some of them are right out in the open. We even call them "shortcomings." That even sounds cruel. You can Google "short jokes" and get 188 million results. This world is not hospitable to the vertically challenged. Today we read about Zacchaeus, who all of us say, "was a wee little man and a wee little man was he." We've made a big deal about how short Zac was—to the point that we miss what Luke is telling us. Luke isn't concerned with his *height*—he is concerned with his *sight*.

 Remember the last few weeks we have been looking at how Luke has told us stories about those who really see Jesus and those who don't? Jesus is almost at Jerusalem, and the time is getting "short." The tension is

"Party with a Purpose"

building. Jesus knows why he's headed there. The disciples think they know why Jesus is headed there. And the crowd is along for the ride. While Jesus is making his final approach to Jerusalem, the persistent widow does "see" Jesus and the Pharisee in the temple doesn't. The tax collector in the temple "sees" Jesus, and so do the little children. The rich ruler won't "see" Jesus; the disciples think they "see" him, but they don't; it's the blind man who does "see" him.

So, Luke isn't all that worried about Zac's size, he's interested in his eyes. It's the rest of the details of Zac's life that are important to Luke and should be important to us as well. Zac is a tax collector, and not just a tax collector, which is bad enough. He is a chief tax collector. He's the one ripping off those who were ripping off others. The Romans had three centers for tax collection in Palestine: Capernaum (where we met Matthew), Jerusalem, and Jericho (which is where Zac lives). Zac is living of the avails of those who are living off the avails—he's a pimp's pimp.

His parents must have been so proud. They named him Zacchaeus which means "pure." This means they had plans for Zac. My parents named me Blayne which means "yellow." I can safely say I've surpassed all their dreams for me. Set the bar low enough and anything is possible.

Luke tells us Zac is rich before he tells us he is short. That should make us think back in two ways. Jesus has just told a story about a tax collector in the temple and he has just encountered a rich man who spit out the hook to become a fisher of men. If we didn't already know how this story ends, we'd be wondering about now—"I wonder which of these ways Zac will go. Will he be like the repentant tax collector and receive forgiveness? Or will he be like the self-righteous rich man who turns Jesus down?"

Jesus is heading through Jericho and there is a lot of excitement. That will happen when you restore sight to someone on the other side of town, and this beggar is jumping all around, praising God. It was all pretty noisy. A crowd gathers. Zac knows Jesus is coming through town, and Luke tells us that "he was seeking to see who Jesus was" (Luke 19:3). Notice the "*seeing*" language there again?

Here's where the shortness thing comes into play. There is this huge crowd around Jesus. This is an issue for Zac, especially when his nose is at everyone's elbow level and they all hate him anyway. They weren't about to let this little "sleeze-ball" through to the front of the line.

Zac hasn't risen to the top by taking no for an answer, so he runs ahead and climbs up in a sycamore fig tree to get a better vantage point.

Sycamore trees grew up to forty feet high. They had thick trunks and sturdy low branches—the perfect perch for paparazzi. He was going to see Jesus, no matter what got in his way.

Jesus gets there and surprises Zac. Zac is up there to see Jesus and now Jesus sees him. That's awkward. The whole story and Zac's plans get turned upside down here. The whole thing starts with Zac seeking to see Jesus and now Jesus sees him and is asking to go to his place for dinner. Zac didn't see that coming. Jesus says, "Zacchaeus, hurry and come down, for I must stay at your house today" (Luke 19:5b). Did you hear that? "I *must* stay at your house today"? Whenever Luke records Jesus using this little word, he is either referring to his own mission—what he must do—or to what God has already planned—what must take place, including his own death and resurrection.

Jesus isn't fooling around here—he's doing this on purpose. He's not going to Zac's house because it would probably be one of the nicest in Jericho, or because he needed some tax advice, or because he wanted a really nice place to rest up before facing the suffering ahead of him in Jerusalem. He was there because he wanted to be there. That was why he was there in Jericho. This was no chance meeting. This was not Jesus calling Zac's bluff. This was Jesus showing us why he came to earth.

So, Zac obeys—he hurries and comes down and offers Jesus generous hospitality. Already something is happening to Zac. Maybe nothing dramatic yet, because it was certainly expected back then if a travelling rabbi wanted to eat at your house, you would spare no expense to show him your finest. But if Zac got to where he was by taking, he's now showing a more open-handed giving.

No one else around sees what is starting to happen. They *see* something, but not that. What they see is Jesus going to the house of a notorious sinner to enjoy a lovely meal that they've probably paid for by the money Zac has stolen from them. So, they start to grumble. We've heard this grumbling before. Back in chapter 15 it's the Pharisees and scribes who are grumbling that Jesus is "receiving sinners and eating with them." That's when Jesus tells those three stories of the lost sheep, the lost coin, and the lost son. When the crowd sees what is happening, their hearts do not expand but they contract into fussy faultfinding. Quite a contrast to what is happening inside the heart of Zacchaeus.

In the midst of the meal, Zac stands up (and all his smart aleck friends say, "*Stand up* Zac!") and says to Jesus, "Behold, Lord ("Lord," just like the

"Party with a Purpose"

blind beggar outside of Jericho), the half of my goods I give to the poor. And if I have defrauded anyone of anything, I restore it fourfold" (Luke 19:8). Something has happened to him. He goes beyond what the Mosaic law requires as far as giving to the poor and making restitution is concerned. He's not obeying the law, he's displaying grace—just like Jesus has displayed to him. He's come to know the freedom of living in extravagant grace. Just like the sinful woman back in chapter 7 when Jesus says, "He who is forgiven little, loves little" (Luke 7:47). Jesus is polite enough not to use "little" language here, but the truth is the same.

The contrast between Zac and the rich ruler should knock us over. The rich ruler was too attached to what he thought was his—his money. And he wouldn't let it go. It had too great a hold on him. It's true that whatever sticks to our hearts tends to stick to our fingers. But Zac just lets this stuff fly. He has come to see what is most important. Great things have happened: the poor are served, the wronged are vindicated, and salvation comes to Zacchaeus and his household since he is a true son of Abraham, part of God's kingdom.

This is the happy ending we're looking for, but it's still not the message of this story. This is not just another story about some unlikely person seeing Jesus as he is. The real point is in what Jesus says in verse 10: "For the Son of Man came to seek and save the lost." So, it's not just a matter of Zac seeing Jesus. The real message is that Jesus sees Zac. As a matter of fact, that's why he came—to seek those just like Zac, just like us, who are lost without him.

This is the abiding truth of this text:
We see Jesus because we are seen by Jesus
We seek Jesus because we are sought by Jesus.

Like everything else, it's not really about us, it's about him. We get it all backwards by focusing on ourselves and our own needs and abilities and gifts and desires. Jesus wants us to focus where he focuses—on those who are lost, on those who don't have what we have already. He is challenging our self-centered focus and is calling us to look beyond ourselves.

There is a complete change that comes with our conversion to Christ and it is something that must be initiated by God and not us, because we can't do it ourselves. We go through this miraculous change from living for ourselves, to dying to ourselves, to being willing to die for Jesus, and then finally being willing to live for Jesus. You might think the order should be reversed—that we should be willing to live for Jesus before we are willing to die for him. That's not the order the Bible places them. Frankly it's a lot harder to be willing to live for Jesus than die for him. It might be more dramatic to be called on to die for him, but it is far more demanding to live for him every day in every situation. Which would you rather do? Make a point or make a difference? Both are important, but we need to keep them in perspective.

Part of that willingness to live for him is to follow his lead in seeking those who are lost. And we seek them, not because we must, but because Jesus first sought us. We *go* because Jesus first *came* to us, we *love* because he *first loved* us. We *serve* because he *first served* us.

Truth be told, he's still serving us. He's standing at his table and inviting us to come—to enjoy his provision, to experience his presence, to remember his dying sacrifice so we might be his living sacrifices.

"It Is Unfinished"

Mark 16:1–8, ESV
March 31, 2013, Easter

Series title: "Mark: Keeping Up with the King"

PRAYER FOR ILLUMINATION

O LORD, our hearts are bursting with the joy that could only come on Easter. The gloom and grief of Friday have burned off and we are living in the light of the resurrection. Shadows have gone and we see the brilliant light of your Son. So may the words of my mouth and the meditations be pleasing in your sight, O LORD, our Rock and our Redeemer. Amen.

SERMON

Have you ever sat through a movie that was entertaining all the way through until you got to the ending and were completely disappointed? Some are like that and, to be honest, it's a bit frustrating. For example, from the list of Top 10 Worst Movie Endings of All Time, you have *Ocean's Eleven* because the way it ended was so cheesy that you just knew they were planning *Ocean's Twelve* and *Thirteen* at least, and maybe more. Then there is *Lord of the Rings: The Return of the King*. The problem here is that the movie didn't end—it went on so long that you were glad there would be no sequel (just a prequel). I'm no Siskel and Ebert or Rotten Tomatoes, but I'm sure you would agree with me when I say a bad ending can spoil the whole movie for us.

Enter Mark and his account of the resurrection. Didn't you feel like he left us hanging? Seriously? This is part of the reason why Mark is the Rodney Dangerfield of the Gospels—he just gets no respect. Why? During the high points of the Christian year, no one reads Mark. How many read Mark at Christmas? Nobody, because Mark doesn't even mention Jesus' birth. And at Easter, how many times have you heard people read Mark's account? Not many. The thing just ends, and we have no record of Jesus appearing to his disciples or commissioning them to spread the good news to ends of the earth.

Just so that we know: pretty near everyone believes Mark's Gospel ends with verse 8. He might have intended to write more, but we don't have it. There are two alternative endings, a long one and a short one, but these probably aren't from Mark. So, this is all we've got. This is not like a home movie where we can choose from a few alternative endings. This is it. Mark starts his Gospel abruptly, but the way it ends is almost shocking. It leaves us longing for closure. What happens with all the loose ends? Will these terrified women actually tell the disciples? Will they meet up with Jesus back in Galilee? Will Jesus tell them to go into all the world and preach the gospel? Some literary critics say Mark does this on purpose because he doesn't like happy endings. Mark is this hip, postmodern cynic who is trying to mess with our heads by leaving everything up in the air. My first response is *ppttthhhh!* But, who knows, maybe they're onto something.

Regardless, it looks like we've drawn the short straw and we get Mark this Easter. That may not be what we expected but that's what this Easter story is all about—it's all about the unexpected.

Not only is this Easter story not what we expected—nothing happens the way these three women expect it either. They head to the tomb expecting the stone to be in place; it isn't. They expect Jesus to be dead; he isn't. They don't expect to see an angel, but they do. They don't expect to get scared out of their jammies and run away in complete confusion and fear, but they do.

What is God saying to us through this unexpected story?

Maybe he's saying it's not about us. We look at these three women and wonder what is going on with them anyway. On Friday they were there at the cross when the rest of the disciples were cowering for cover. Now they leave the empty tomb all freaked out and disobey what the angel tells them to do. He says, "Go tell," and they say, "*Aaahhh!*" And they don't tell anyone. Frankly, that's disappointing.

But let's face it, the people who follow Jesus all through Mark's Gospel are not a very impressive lot. They are dull, they fail more than they succeed, they are full of themselves, they are . . . just like us. We've seen this as

"It Is Unfinished"

we've worked our way through this Gospel. It's an important reminder to see Mark is never wanting to draw attention to us as much as he is drawing attention to Jesus. This is Jesus' story, not ours. He's the headliner. It is a very real temptation every time we look at a passage of Scripture, to look immediately for how it relates to us. Why is that? Sometimes it's because we really do want to learn from Scripture and we don't want it just to be an academic exercise. But most often, we head too quickly for applying Scripture because we are preoccupied with ourselves. As though the main thing about any text is what it tells us is our own responsibility.

This story tells us what happens when we think everything depends on us: chaos, disorder, failure, disobedience. This story doesn't tell us about our responsibility—it tells us about our response. There is a world of difference between the two. Responsibility tells us what we're supposed to do on our own steam, our own initiative. Response tells us what we can do as we trust in the risen Christ. It's a matter of focus. This story is about him, and we are part of it as we join his story, not by asking him to join ours. So, whatever this story is about, it's not about our responsibility, it's about our response—and we probably weren't expecting that.

Speaking of our response, maybe God is also saying this story is all about faith. Do you notice the women don't see the resurrection itself? As a matter of fact, no Gospel writer records anyone actually seeing the resurrection take place. What do the women see? They see nothing. And right where they expected to see someone. Jesus was supposed to be there, and he was gone.

How are these women to know the resurrection had taken place? They have to trust the angel's word is true. Maybe they had heard Jesus when he told his followers that he'd been delivered over to death but would rise from the dead. If that's the case, they'd still have to trust what Jesus said. Think about it for a minute. The angel says Jesus has been raised because he isn't laying there in the tomb anymore. Is this the only explanation that fits the situation? I could tell you that all the pink elephants have flown to Florida for the winter and then prove it to you by asking, "So do you see any pink elephants around? See?"

Faith is not the only possible response. And for these women, at least for now, it isn't their response either. They chose to run away in fear. That's not all that hard to understand—they were standing inside a tomb in the middle of a graveyard, and they were talking to an angel. What is the first thing every angel has to say? "Fear not!" We're not that different. If we were in their sandals, we'd probably come unglued just like them.

The angel said the two things that should have built up faith in these women: "Don't be alarmed," and "He has been raised" (Mark 16:6). But they respond with fear rather than faith. Faith can only come with help from the risen Christ. Easter is actually a scary place until their fear can be replaced by faith. It is no different for us.

Could there be even more that we don't expect from Easter? Maybe God is trying to tell us it's about second chances. The angel says to the women, "But go tell his disciples and Peter that he is going before you to Galilee. There you will see him, just as he told you" (Mark 16:7). This is more than a fulfillment of what Jesus says in chapter 14:28: "But after I am raised up, I will go before you to Galilee." This tells us Jesus still hasn't given up on his followers, no matter how much they had given up on him. What a picture of forgiveness and death-defying love! After all that's happened, Easter brings a new day. Failures can be forgiven, and despair can be turned into joy. It's back to normal—Jesus is on the road, ahead of his followers, and he's calling them to follow after him again.

Notice who gets singled out—Peter. Of all the disciples who deserted Jesus, Peter made the biggest boasts about standing true until the death, and he was the one who deliberately denied knowing Jesus three times. Not only is there hope when we mess up, but there is hope when we mess up big time. Maybe you came today not expecting to hear that.

Maybe God's got something else to tell us—still something more we hadn't expected. Maybe he's saying it's his resurrection not his return. You probably didn't expect that because it sounds a bit strange. Of course, it's not his return. Easter is a celebration of his resurrection, not his second coming. But sometimes I'm not so sure we've got this straight.

We need to remember what this day means in God's larger story. Easter is not the end of the story, it's just the beginning of the end. We can get into all kinds of trouble when we confuse the two.

Christ is risen, but the women still run from the empty tomb in fear. Christ is risen, and we are able to walk in the power of the resurrection, but there is still injustice, oppression, sickness, and death in this world. Christ is risen, and the church is empowered to grow in unity and witness, but there is still so much left to do. Christ is risen—that is for the past and the present—but his return is still in the future. Easter is a celebration, but it's not celebrating the end of our mission, just the beginning.

"It Is Unfinished"

Easter is a lot of things—some we expect and some we didn't expect. And Mark helps us by the way he ends this story so abruptly and unexpectedly. He helps us push toward our own ending. Just when we'd like to put the cork in the bottle and say, "It is finished," Mark pops the cork and assures us, "It is unfinished!" The last part of the Easter story has not yet been written, because each of us and all of us are still writing it. Maybe that's the most unexpected thing of all. The message of Easter is meant to take us by surprise.

Humorist Phil Callaway was talking about driving by a cemetery with his son Steve, when Steve was only five years old. Someone had just dug a new grave and Steve pointed his finger at the pile of dirt and the hole in the ground and said, "Look, Dad, one got out!"

That's the story of Easter. Mark tells us in just eight verses: "Look guys, One got out!" And he trusts us to take it from there.

One of the ways we have celebrated the living Christ is to meet together around his table. That is how we will conclude our worship time this morning, but even this is not the end, only the beginning of the end.

"Emmaus Always Happens"

Luke 24:13–35, ESV

June 29, 2014

Series Title: "What on Earth is God Up To?"

PRAYER FOR ILLUMINATION

LORD, so many times we're like these two disciples and you have joined us in our journe; we are none the wiser for it. Forgive us those times when we live like you have not been raised and we are left to figure out life on our own steam. So may the words of my mouth and the meditations of all our hearts be pleasing in your sight, O LORD, our Rock and our Redeemer. Amen.

SERMON

It's vacation time. What that normally means is that we are really excited to get where we're going. It's the trip back that's little boring and anti-climactic. Usually getting there is the fun part, going back—not so much. Unless, of course, you're the goalie for the hapless Macrorie hockey team. I grew up near the bustling metropolis of Macrorie—population abou eighty-six, if you counted house pets. Our town had what every prairie town had—a hockey rink. What we didn't have were hockey players. You won't find a sign on the outskirts of Macrorie: "Home of Such and Such an NHL hockey player." We did produce one Rhodes Scholar, but I can't even remember his name. After all, this is the prairies. I had the dubious honor of being the team goalie. This was a tough job. Our goal each game was to keep the shot totals under three

"Emmaus Always Happens"

digits. The upside was that I always got a great tan all winter from the goal light going off.

There's a book on every goalie—rating their strengths and weaknesses. The book on me was that I was big, so I covered a lot of the net and I had a decent glove hand. That was it—I had one glove hand. I was the Michael Jackson of goalies. And "I was bad, real bad!" So, what that meant for me was I dreaded the drive to the games, sometimes was even physically nauseated, because I knew I was going to get lit up. But the ride home was always better, because the game was over. I was much happier on the way back.

That is much the same as our two disciples in our story this morning. They seem pretty miserable as they head out from Jerusalem that first Easter Sunday. There's some mystery to this story—Luke leaves out some details that we would probably like to know. Like, who was the other disciple? Cleopas and whom? No one knows. Some suggest Cleopas is the same as the Clopas in John's Gospel. Clopas was married to Mary, the sister of Jesus' mother whose name, of course, was also Mary. (This is my sister Mary and my other sister Mary.) Mary was at the foot of the cross with the other women. And if this was the case, these two disciples were Jesus' Uncle Clopas and Aunt Mary. They may indeed have been husband and wife because Luke says they were talking and "discussing" together. "Discussing" means to debate strongly—in other words, arguing. It wasn't that Cleopas had taken the wrong road out of Jerusalem and wouldn't stop for directions—they were debating over what had just happened over the past few days, including that very day.

From the way Luke describes them, they seem pretty depressed and upset. Luke says they stood there, looking sad. They remind me of Eeyore—the rather downcast donkey from Winnie the Pooh. What is important to know is these two are on a journey, and it's while you're on a journey that God reveals truth to his followers—like all through Luke's Gospel. Well, these two are about to get the revelation of a lifetime, but they don't even know it. That's not too abnormal. Jesus' disciples seldom "get it" even when he tells them straight up.

The other thing we need to remember is that Luke tells the story of Jesus' resurrection in stages—because his own followers are having such a hard time coming to grips with a crucified and resurrected Messiah. Remember last week they were to believe in the resurrection because of the empty tomb and remembering what Jesus had told them about being crucified and then raised from the dead. Some got it—the women. Some didn't get it—Peter and the rest of the apostles.

Now, Jesus is turning it up a notch. He's actually appearing to his followers in person. And guess what—they still don't get it. But, they don't get it because Jesus doesn't want them to get it—yet. Luke says, "their eyes were kept from recognizing him" (Luke 24:16). What is Jesus up to?

He joins in on the conversation and falls into step with them as they're walking along. He "innocently" asks them what they're talking about. The response of Cleopas is classic. He says, "Are you the only visitor to Jerusalem who does not know the things that have happened there in these days?" (Luke 24:18b). Isn't that hilarious? I'm sure even today in paradise, they're still razzing Cleopas about this. "Hey, Cleo, remember the time you made fun of Jesus for not knowing about his own resurrection?" Talk about sweet irony!

Anyway, Jesus plays dumb with these two who don't need to play—it's real. He asks about what has been happening and Cleopas spills it all.

> Concerning Jesus of Nazareth, a man who was a prophet mighty in deed and word before God and all the people, and how our chief priests and rulers delivered him up to be condemned to death and crucified him. But we had hoped that he was the one to redeem Israel. Yes, and besides all this, it is now the third day since these things happened. Moreover, some women of our company amazed us. They were at the tomb early in the morning, and when they did not find his body, they came back saying that they had even seen a vision of angels, who said he was alive. Some of those who were with us went to the tomb and found it just as the women had said, but him they did not see. (Luke 24:19–24).

At this point, we're wondering what must be going through Jesus' mind as these two are talking. They obviously don't get it. They're waiting for a Messiah who will overthrow Rome and restore Israel to prominence. And having their Messiah die just didn't fit their paradigm. Their Messiah would be a victor not a victim.

Jesus steps in with some pretty pointed words. Remember, each time the followers of Jesus are faced with the resurrection, someone gets bawled out for not getting it? Last week it was the women at the tomb. This week, it's these two. "O foolish ones, and slow of heart to believe all that the prophets have spoken! Was it not necessary [there's that 'necessary' word again] that the Christ should suffer these things and enter into his glory?" (Luke 24:26).

"Emmaus Always Happens"

They didn't understand that Jesus' road to glory had to go through suffering first, so he could accomplish his mission of bringing complete salvation to us all. So, Jesus takes this opportunity to explain to them how this was part of God's plan since the beginning.

What he does is spend the rest of the journey explaining to these two how all through the Old Testament, this very thing was predicted. How the Scriptures pointed to himself—his death and resurrection. We can only imagine what it must have been like to have Jesus himself explain himself from the Scriptures. How much tuition would you pay to get that lecture? It didn't give them a headache, but it did give them some strange heartburn. They still didn't know they were getting the lesson of a lifetime—not until they stopped for supper.

These two insisted that Jesus join them for supper and it's when Jesus takes the bread, breaks it, blesses it, and gives it to them that, all of a sudden, the blinders fall off. It's like Jesus finally says, "OK, now!" Luke says, "their eyes were opened, and they recognized him" (Luke 24:31). That's all they needed, and then Jesus was gone. Jesus knew they needed to see him alive, but he also knew they needed to understand why he was crucified and raised from the dead. Then, and only then, could their whole lives be turned around by this surprising new truth. The only other time Luke records these same words is when Jesus feeds the five thousand back in chapter 9.

The change is drastic. On the journey out, they looked like Eeyore, but now they look like Tigger. They can't wait until morning, so they head back to Jerusalem because they can't wait to tell the apostles and all the rest this good news. There is no comparison between the two journeys. They get to Jerusalem and find out that Jesus has also, sometime in this same day, appeared to Peter. The same group that thought the women were out of their mind, were out of their own minds with joy: "The Lord has risen indeed!" (Luke 24:34).

So, we get to the end of the story and ask ourselves, "What did Luke want to teach us about the risen Christ?" And it's simpler than we think. Luke didn't tell us this story to impress on us how we are to read the Old Testament, or to show us the importance of the Lord's Supper. He tells us this story simply to remind us of one thing: The risen Christ gives new life to us. Our lives are never the same when we encounter the risen Jesus. He turns us from sad to glad, from darkness to light, from depression to elation, from Eeyore to Tigger. These two disciples didn't think the same way, walk the same way, or act the same way. It all changed with the risen Jesus. It had the same effect on the entire church back then—as it should for us today.

So, with this in mind, we turn again to our three life-changing questions:

What on earth has gone wrong? We also have a problem believing the resurrection—but ours is not that same as theirs back then. They had trouble believing the resurrection was true. Today we have trouble believing it matters. Our lives do not look like the ones who follow a risen Savior. It's easy for us to think it is business as usual. We live our lives, we conduct our business, we relate to others as though the resurrection hasn't made a lick of difference. We should start each day with the confession: "He is risen, he is risen indeed!" not "I'm awake, I'm awake indeed!" That's part of what on earth has gone wrong.

What on earth is God up to? God is up to showing us the difference the resurrection makes for each and all of us. Remember last week—we were called to believe the resurrection because of what they didn't see and what they didn't remember. This week we're called to believe because we see the risen Christ. God still has something up his sleeve, but we're going to have to wait until next week to find out what it is as we conclude our study of Luke's Gospel.

How on earth can we be the church in this new space? The church is the community of the resurrection, it is the fellowship of new life—eternal life. So, the church needs to reflect this truth. We need to exude, ooze, overflow, bubble over with life. When people look at the church, are they blown away by the sheer energy of new life empowered by the resurrection of Christ? Truth be told, a lot of people look at us in the church as a whole herd of Eeyores. People who can find the storm in any silver lining. That needs to change—now. Our encounter with the risen Christ has given us new life. This is no time for grumping and groaning and moaning about everything. Christ is risen! It's Tigger time!

"Prison Break"

Acts 16:16–40, ESV
January 18, 2015

Series Title: "Living the Mission"

PRAYER FOR ILLUMINATION

LORD, we thank you for giving us what we could never have gained on our own—the gift of being your forgiven family—each of us a loved son or daughter and all of us a diverse family of faith. Help us understand what it means to have been saved and the difference that makes in all our lives. And may the words of my mouth and the meditations of all our hearts be pleasing in your sight, O LORD, our Rock and our Redeemer. Amen.

SERMON

We've all heard those jokes that start with: "You know you're a _____ when you _____." Like you know you're a redneck when you have to move your car's transmission before you can take a bath, or when you've hit a deer with your car—on purpose. Or you know you're a college student when caffeine has replaced vegetables in the four major food groups. Or you know you're a pastor when you can't be in a crowd without wanting to take an offering. Or you know you're from Caronport when you drive into Moose Jaw with ten dollars in one hand and the Ten Commandments in the other and don't want to break either one.

But what if we were to say, "You know you're saved when . . . "? Then all of a sudden, the room gets quiet. We all know being saved should make a difference—that being saved is kind of like being pregnant—pretty soon it should start to show. But that still leaves us with the question, "How does it show?" Luke helps us here with this story in Acts 16. Paul and Silas are on what we call the second missionary journey. They are joined by Luke and Timothy by the time they step on European soil for the first time. Maybe you're like me, and when we hear "Europe" we think about high culture and sophistication. Philippi is in Northern Greece—Macedonia—but Luke's picture of this place is far from flattering. It sounds very pagan, brutish, and inhospitable to say the least. It sounds like a place very proud of itself and closed to outsiders as their inferiors. Not particularly high class, when you think about it.

There isn't enough Jewish influence in Philippi for it to have its own synagogue, so Paul and his missionary group gather at the river where some women have gathered to pray. Lydia, a wealthy businesswoman from Asia, is the first to receive Christ; she persuades Paul and his pals to stay at her house. Here's where we pick up Luke's story. They are heading down to the place of prayer when they are shadowed by this slave girl who is possessed by a spirit of divination. This girl is yelling out loud, "These men are servants of the Most High God, who proclaim to you the way of salvation" (Acts 16:17). At first, we might think, "What a great answer to prayer! Free publicity! Paul doesn't have to take out a full-page ad in the Philippi Free Press—this is priceless!" But there's more at play here than free publicity. After a few days of being stalked by this looney loudspeaker, Paul has had enough. He swings around on his heels and says to the spirit, "I command you in the name of Jesus Christ to come out of her"(Acts 16:18b). And the spirit leaves.

Something significant has happened here. Paul doesn't allow Satan to publicize his identity just like Jesus did back in Luke 4 and 8. But there's more to this announcement and more to this slave girl than that. She is yelling about them being servants of the Most High God. But she didn't know what that meant nor did anyone else in Philippi. No one would have connected the Most High God with Yahweh—most of them would have thought of Zeus. And what does it mean to be saved? The notion of being saved in the Greco-Roman world was to be rescued or delivered from some bad situation like a disease or personal trouble. It didn't mean to be forgiven of sin and given a place in God's family and kingdom. So, this announcement wasn't such a bonus after all. And the ironic thing about it is that if there is ever a person who needed to be saved, it was this slave girl herself. Luke doesn't give us her name (we'll call her Meg—short for

"Prison Break"

Megaphone), but he does describe her for us. She is a girl doubly enslaved in need of release. She has been enslaved to this spirit of divination and we also find out she is enslaved to a group of greedy entrepreneurs who are prophecy pimps. She is a person made in God's image, and they treat her like a human horoscope, or worse yet, a cash cow, a possession to be used for their profit. If anyone needed to be saved, it was Meg. If anyone needed to be freed, it was her, and in the name of Jesus Christ she received what she could never have earned—her freedom, her "salvation."

All this did not go unnoticed by her handlers. There goes their ticket to Easy Street and they're upset. So, what do they do? They grab Paul and Silas (I guess Luke and Timothy had gone out to buy some Greek yogurt) and they follow the traffic to the marketplace in the middle of town and bring them before the authorities. Notice the charges they lay against them. They don't say, "These guys messed up our human trafficking operation." They say, "These men are Jews, and they are disturbing our city. They advocate customs that are not lawful for us as Romans to accept or practice." They spin the charges to appeal to the prejudices of the rulers and the crowd. The crowd very soon turns ugly and the rulers have Paul and Silas stripped and beaten publicly with rods by the police. Then they are thrown in jail with orders given to keep them in maximum security lock down. Quite a sight! Here you have a city full of free Roman citizens who are violent, arrogant, xenophobic (afraid of strangers), and abusers of human rights. Sometimes you can look like you are free and not be free at all.

But the reverse is also true. Sometimes you can look like you're completely imprisoned but, in reality, you couldn't be any freer. Paul and Silas are in the dark, dank inner cell where terrible things happen, feet in wooden stocks, but they could not be freer. Contrast this to the jailer, probably a former Roman soldier, who feels free enough to snooze on the job. But just having the keys to someone else's cell doesn't make you free. And being locked up in a cell doesn't mean you're not. Luke has mentioned several times already in the book of Acts that prisons weren't permanent for the apostles. The apostles had bad grammar—they would start sentences and not finish them. God kept breaking them out. It's a bit like the angry teenage inmate who yells at the guards, "You can keep my body locked up but you can't keep my face from breaking out!"

So here are Paul and Silas in jail at midnight, their feet in stocks, their backs swollen and bleeding, praying and singing hymns. The rest of the prisoners are listening—what else could they do? They were a captive audience, right? But notice—their feet may have been locked in stocks, but their tongues were freed to pray and to praise. That's real freedom.

We're all waiting for what happens next aren't we? Maybe you've heard the saying that old jailers never die, their cells just deteriorate? Apparently, this jailer hadn't heard that one because he had drifted off to sleep when God wakes him up with his own version of "Jailhouse Rock." The cell doors pop open and the shackles fall off—the place is "All Shook Up." Uh-huh. Immediately the jailer thinks Elvis has left the building—and taken everyone else with him. This pagan jailer sees that the "gods are upset with him," and he fears the same from his superiors, so he decides to end it himself. Paul shouts out "Do not harm yourself, for we are all here" (Acts 16:28). Now who is imprisoned and who is free? We see the jailer as he is—really: fearful, captive to superstition, aware of his own powerlessness. He falls at the freed feet of Paul and Silas and asks, "Sirs, what must I do to be saved?" I dream of people coming up and asking me this very same question. But we need to understand it in the way the jailer means it. He really doesn't know anything about the one true God or his way of salvation through his Son Jesus Christ. He just knows he needs help to escape from where he finds himself. N. T. Wright translates this question more accurately: "Gentlemen, will you please tell me how I can get out of this mess?"[2] They can. "Believe in the Lord Jesus, and you will be saved, you and your household" (Acts 16:31). They do. The jailer and all his household are baptized right then. And they show gracious hospitality to Paul and Silas—dressing their wounds and giving them food. Pretty hospitable for such an inhospitable place. As a matter of fact, Luke shows the only hospitable places in Philippi are the homes of these new believers. First Lydia's household and now the jailer's. Why? Because they are all rejoicing that they had trusted Jesus.

The story ends the next day when the rulers feel that they have taught these rabble rousers a sufficient lesson and so sent the police to the jailer with orders for their release. Just one more item on a long to-do list—not worth their personal attention. They are rulers of a free Roman city. Busy people—people to meet, chariots to catch—no need to bother with yesterday's news. That is until Paul informs the police he and Silas are Roman citizens and were illegally beaten and imprisoned. This was obviously against Roman law and the rulers could face serious punishment for their actions. Again, we have to ask, "Who is free here and who is not?"

---

2. Wright, *Acts for Everyone*, 67.

"Prison Break"

This is a pretty strange story, full of twists, turns, and ironies. Luke seems to be saying that those who seem to look like they're free actually are not at all. And the ones who don't look like they're free, are. We have a city full of free citizens who are actually enslaved to their own self-preoccupation and can riot at the drop of a hat. We have rulers who pass hasty judgment on others but cower in fear of their own superiors. We have human traffickers who are addicted to their own greed and will do anything to the truth to get revenge.

In contrast to these we have those who are free even though they don't look like it. Obviously, there's Paul and Silas—but they were always free, weren't they? We tend to think this story is about their prison break, but I don't think so, really. There are two other prison breaks in this story—Meg the slave girl and the jailer. They started this story very much enslaved but ended it freed indeed.

So, we go back to our question of a few minutes ago: How do we know we are saved? We know we are saved because we are free—we are freed from sin through Christ and we are freed to serve Christ. We are saved because we are free, and it shows.

James Davison Hunter writes about those who have changed the world for the cause of Christ. He mentions one lady who served as a checkout clerk at a grocery store. She made it her practice to show the love of Christ to all who came through her checkout line. Her sphere of influence was only six square feet, but she made a lasting impact. She knew their names, asked about their lives and families. She volunteered to be praying for them. The lines at her checkout were always way longer than the rest, but these people didn't mind at all. Eventually she retired and passed away a few years later. There was standing room only at her funeral as countless people stood up to share how she had changed their lives. We don't have to be famous or influential to show we are saved or to make a difference. We just allow the grace that has freed us to flow through to someone else.

Appendix

PREACHING DISCURSIVE BIBLICAL TEXTS

"Catching Up to Our Calling"
Philippians 1:27–30

Textual Form: Paranaesis.

Textual DVD: God grants salvation, faith, and suffering.

Textual DNA: The tendency to interpret suffering as abandonment by God rather than his gift to share as believers.

Textual Focus: Paul exhorted the Philippians, "Live like worthy citizens of the gospel!"

Textual Function: To encourage the Philippians to remain true to their calling even in the midst of suffering.

Textual Feel: Encouraging.

Sermon Form: Deductive.

Sermon Focus: Live like worthy citizens of the gospel of Christ.

Sermon Function: To encourage the congregation to remain true to the gospel in the midst of opposition and suffering.

Sermon Feel: Encouraging.

"Bad News About the Good News"
Galatians 1:1–10

Textual Form: Epistolary greeting and exordium (introduction) and rebuke.

Appendix

Textual DVD: God has desired that we be saved and has sent Jesus to save us. He will be praised for what he has done and judge those who distort his gospel.

Textual DNA: The human tendency to disregard God's provisions for salvation by preferring our own versions of the gospel.

Textual Focus: Paul greeted the Galatians by highlighting the importance of remaining true to the gospel he preached to them.

Textual Function: To warn the Galatians of the consequences of deserting the gospel.

Textual Feel: Authoritative, angry.

Sermon Form: Deductive.

Sermon Focus: It's all about the gospel—nothing more, nothing less, nothing else.

Sermon Function: To call the congregation to a dedication to the gospel that will keep us from falling for distortions of it.

Sermon Feel: Aggressive exhortation.

"God's Gospel"
Galatians 1:11–24

Textual Form: Autobiography.

Textual DVD: God has called and saved Paul to be a preacher of the true gospel.

Textual DNA: The need for salvation and a purpose in life.

Textual Focus: Paul informed the Galatians how God used the gospel to transform his own life.

Textual Function: To convince the Galatians of the divine power of the gospel.

Textual Feel: Vulnerable, confessional.

Sermon Form: Inductive.

Sermon Focus: The gospel comes from God, but spreads through us.

Sermon Function: To inspire the congregation to live out their own gospel purposes.

Sermon Feel: Inspirational.

"Gospel Glue"
Galatians 2:1–10

Textual Form: Autobiography.

Textual DVD: God is sovereign and gives a diversity of gifts to his people.

Textual DNA: The tendency to assert our unique gift at the expense of unity.

Textual Focus: Paul informed the Galatians about how the Jerusalem leaders accepted his gospel message.

Textual Function: To convince the Galatians of the authority of his gospel message.

Textual Feel: Challenging.

Sermon Form: Inductive.

Sermon Focus: God's one gospel makes us one free people.

Sermon Function: To show the congregation how the one gospel frees us to serve as we are gifted.

Sermon Feel: Challenging.

"Two Ways of Walking"
Galatians 5:13—6:10

Textual Form: Paranaesis with vice and virtue lists.

Textual DVD: God will not be mocked; Christ has a law and a people; the Spirit produces fruit, eternal life, and leads believers.

Textual DNA: The temptation to abuse freedom in Christ to live according to one's own fleshly desires.

Textual Focus: Paul urged the Galatians, "Walk by the Spirit and not by the flesh!"

Textual Function: To maintain the unity of the church by urging an appropriate Spirit-led lifestyle.

Textual Feel: Urgent, hopeful, authoritative.

Sermon Form: Deductive.

Sermon Focus: Don't walk alone!

Sermon Function: To help the congregation grasp the difference it makes when we live by the Spirit and not by our own sinful desires.

Sermon Feel: Challenging.

"This World is Not Our Home"
1 John 2:12–17

Textual Form: Parenthetical and poetic paranaesis

Textual DVD: God is our Father; he has given us his Word and has from the beginning.

Textual DNA: The need to focus on God when the temptations of the world press in on us.

Textual Focus: John wrote to the church to urge them, "Love God and not the world!"

Textual Function: To encourage the believers to keep loving God rather than what the world offers.

Textual Feel: Encouraging, challenging.

Sermon Form: Inductive-deductive.

Sermon Focus: Love the One who gives you life!

Sermon Function: To encourage the congregation to remain faithful to their love of God in the midst of the world's distractions.

Sermon Feel: Encouraging.

"It's All in the Family"
1 John 3:11–24

Textual Form: Epideictic Rhetorical Maxims (sententiae).

Textual DVD: God is greater than our hearts; he abides in us and gives us his Spirit. Christ laid down his life for us. The Holy Spirit assures us of God's abiding in us.

Textual DNA: The lack of confidence that undermines one's sense of security in the faith and one's desire to live as God desires.

Textual Focus: John encouraged the believers to love each other out of the confidence that comes from abiding in God.

Textual Function: To encourage the believers to act out of the assurance that God dwells/abides in them.

Textual Feel: Challenging and assuring.

Sermon Form: Inductive.

Sermon Focus: Because God lives in us, we can live for each other.

Sermon Function: To encourage the congregation to love each other out of their assurance of God's indwelling.

Sermon Feel: Challenging, assuring.

"A Dream of Irresistible Influence"
Matthew 5:13–16

Textual Form: Metaphors.

Textual DVD: God is glorified when we influence the world through good deeds.

Textual DNA: The difficulty in living up to one's identity and purpose in the kingdom of heaven.

Textual Focus: Jesus called his disciples to influence the world to the glory of God.

Textual Function: To encourage his disciples to live up to their identity and purpose.

Textual Feel: Encouraging, inspiring.

Sermon Form: Inductive.

Sermon Focus: When we show the world who we are, the world will see who God is.

Sermon Function: To encourage the congregation to affect the world for God's glory.

Sermon Feel: Encouraging, inspiring.

Appendix

"A Dream of Real Righteousness"
Matthew 5:17–20

Textual Form: Deliberative, rhetorical proposition.

Textual DVD: God has given his Law which Jesus has come to bring to fulfillment.

Textual DNA: The temptation to put one's own "spin" to God's requirements for us.

Textual Focus: Jesus told his disciples that he came to fulfill the Law.

Textual Function: To remind his disciples of how he brings fulfillment to what God wants his followers to do.

Textual Feel: Authoritative, warning, exhorting.

Sermon Form: Deductive.

Sermon Focus: Find your "rightness" in Jesus' fullness.

Sermon Function: To remind the congregation that we are to do what is right because of our relationship with Jesus.

Sermon Feel: Exhorting.

"A Dream of Intentional Obedience"
Matthew 7:24–29

Textual Form: Deliberative, rhetorical epilogue.

Textual DVD: Jesus has authority that is far greater than human teachers.

Textual DNA: The temptation to hear and not obey.

Textual Focus: Jesus called his disciples to obey what he has told them.

Textual Function: To press his disciples into obeying his teachings.

Textual Feel: Exhorting, challenging.

Sermon Form: Inductive.

Sermon Focus: Just do it!

Sermon Function: To call the congregation to active obedience of what Jesus calls us to be and do.

Sermon Feel: Exhorting, challenging.

Appendix

PREACHING POETIC BIBLICAL TEXTS

"Kiss the Risen Son!"
Psalm 2

Textual Form: Royal psalm.

Textual DVD: God is in heaven, ruling in majestic wrath and judgment, possesses all nations, adopts his anointed one.

Textual DNA: The tendency to rebel against God. The need to fear God, serve him and take refuge in him.

Textual Focus: The psalmist called on the readers to acknowledge the power of God's anointed king.

Textual Function: To motivate all to acknowledge God's anointed one.

Textual Feel: Somewhat derisive and mocking, sobering.

Sermon Form: Inductive.

Sermon Focus: You don't mess with the Messiah!

Sermon Function: To call the congregation to worship the risen Christ.

Sermon Feel: From ironic mocking to majestic call to worship.

"A Wedding Fit for a King"
Psalm 45

Textual Form: Epithalomion

Textual DVD: God is powerful, majestic. He has chosen the King and promises him a legacy.

Textual DNA: The need for a strong savior who is mighty to save.

Textual Focus: The psalmist called all worshippers to celebrate the wedding of the king.

Textual Function: To celebrate the majesty of the king and the beauty of his bride.

Textual Feel: Celebratory, joyful.

Sermon Form: Inductive.

Sermon Focus: Amen, Come Lord Jesus!

Sermon Function: To encourage the congregation to live in the anticipation of Jesus' second coming.

Sermon Feel: Celebratory, joyful, anticipatory.

"When We Feel Depressed"
Psalms 42–43

Textual Form: Personal laments.

Textual DVD: God may seem distant yet shows steadfast love that inspires hope.

Textual DNA: The need for hope of deliverance when one feels forgotten and cast down.

Textual Focus: The psalmist called the readers to hope in God when times were bleak.

Textual Function: The psalmist called himself to hope in God even in the most difficult of circumstances.

Textual Feel: Predominately mournful with a refrain of hope.

Sermon Form: Inductive with a refrain.

Sermon Focus: Nobody knows the trouble I've seen—nobody knows but Jesus.

Sermon Function: To encourage the congregation to hope in Jesus even in the midst of the most difficult circumstances.

Sermon Feel: From hopeless to helpless to hopeful

"When We Feel Surrounded"
Psalm 12

Textual Form: Communal lament.

Textual DVD: God can speak, can save, and can act.

Textual DNA: The temptation to give up or strike out in anger when one feels alone and outnumbered.

Textual Focus: The psalmist called on readers to trust in God's protection even while surrounded by evil.

Textual Function: To persuade the readers to trust the pure word of the LORD.

Textual Feel: Anxious, depressed, until verse 5, then hopeful.

Sermon Form: Inductive.

Sermon Focus: God has spoken, and his word is pure.

Sermon Function: To encourage the congregation to trust God's word of deliverance when surrounded by evil.

Sermon Feel: Anxious then hopeful.

"When We are Betrayed by a Friend"
Psalm 55

Textual Form: Individual lament.

Textual DVD: God hears one's complaints, can save and will bring justice.

Textual DNA: The need to trust in God rather than fight or flight when betrayed by a close friend.

Textual Focus: The psalmist trusted in the LORD when betrayed by a close friend.

Textual Function: The psalmist wants the readers to trust God in the midst of betrayal rather than take matters into their own hands.

Textual Feel: Deep hurt, devastation, moving into trust.

Sermon Form: Inductive.

Sermon Focus: We can trust Jesus, even when we can't trust anyone else.

Sermon Function: To point the congregation to trust in God rather than their own resources when dealing with deep, personal betrayal.

Sermon Feel: An emotional rollercoaster leading to a declaration of trust.

"A Whole New Kind of Hero"
Isaiah 42:1–9

Textual Form: Salvation oracle.

Textual DVD: God gave his Spirit, created the earth, called his people to be a light to the nations, and shared his glory with no other.

APPENDIX

Textual DNA: The need for God's people to know he had a plan for them and they could trust him in it.

Textual Focus: God revealed his servant to his people.

Textual Function: To show God's people his plans for them.

Textual Feel: Majestic.

Sermon Form: Deductive.

Sermon Function: To call the congregation to a new level of servant leadership

Sermon Focus: What God wants in a leader is a servant.

Sermon Feel: Inspiring, inquisitive.

"What Happens When God Colors Outside the Lines?"
Isaiah 44:24–45:13

Textual Form: Declarative praise/salvation oracle.

Textual DVD: God is Creator, Sustainer, Redeemer, sovereign, plans for the deliverance of his people, is without equal, and the Holy One of Israel.

Textual DNA: The human tendency to assume God will work out his plans in ways that make sense to them and to doubt him if he does not.

Textual Focus: Isaiah reminded Israel of God's sovereign capacity to work his purposes in surprising ways.

Textual Function: To call Israel to praise God for his deliverance of his people in way they had never imagined.

Textual Feel: Awe-inspiring, surprising.

Sermon Form: Inductive.

Sermon Focus: Our God is entirely faithful but completely unpredictable.

Sermon Function: To call the congregation to worship God in all his surprising ways of bringing us deliverance.

Sermon Feel: Awe-inspiring, surprising.

"Extreme Makeover: David's House Edition"
Amos 9:11–15

Textual Form: Salvation oracle.

Textual DVD: God is a gracious provider for his people.

Textual DNA: God's people needed a savior who would reverse their fortunes and bring restoration.

Textual Focus: God promised future restoration/renewal for his people Israel.

Textual Function: To give Israel the motivation to turn from their sinful ways and seek the LORD.

Textual Feel: Assuring, inspiring, hopeful.

Sermon Form: Inductive.

Sermon Focus: The new is only for those who are made new.

Sermon Function: To spur the congregation to obedience and enhance their expectation of God's blessing of renewal.

Sermon Feel: Inspirational, hopeful.

"Why Do You Reject Our Worship?"
Malachi 2:10–16

Textual Form: Disputation speech.

Textual DVD: God is a covenant-maker, Creator, and the judge of those who are unfaithful to his covenant.

Textual DNA: To remind Israel that worship was not going through the motions and performing the right rituals but comes from covenant faithfulness.

Textual Focus: Malachi called Israel to faithful, obedient worship.

Textual Function: To help Israel see the hypocrisy of worship that did not come out of covenant faithfulness.

Textual Feel: Warning, confrontational.

Sermon Form: Deductive.

Sermon Focus: Worship starts with who we are not with what we do.

Sermon Function: To encourage pure motivation in worship among those in the congregation.

Sermon Feel: Confrontational, exhorting.

Appendix

"How Are We Robbing You?"
Malachi 3:6–12

Textual Form: Disputation speech.

Textual DVD: God is faithful to his covenant, just in his judgments, and gracious in his blessings.

Textual DNA: The temptation to be miserly in their approach to their holy and gracious God.

Textual Focus: YHWH was calling Israel to repentance through the faithful giving of their tithes.

Textual Function: To call Israel to repent of their stinginess and to give their tithes generously and joyfully.

Textual Feel: Warning that turns into promise.

Sermon Form: Inductive-deductive.

Sermon Focus: If we love God greatly, we will give to him generously.

Sermon Function: To call the congregation to express their love to God by giving generously to him.

Sermon Feel: Urging, anticipating.

PREACHING NARRATIVE BIBLICAL TEXTS:

"Why Did God Test Abraham?"
Genesis 22:1–19

Textual Form: Test narrative.

Textual DVD: God is the one who tested his followers and provided for them.

Textual DNA: The temptation to find personal solutions to our difficult situations rather than being obedient to what God requires.

Textual Focus: Abraham's faith in God's ability to provide was tested.

Textual Function: To encourage Israel to be faithful in her own times of testing.

Textual Feel: Suspenseful.

Sermon Form: Narrative.

Appendix

Sermon Focus: Will it be DIY or will it be "Here am I"?

Sermon Function: To encourage the congregation to trust God even in situations when it does not make sense.

Sermon Feel: Suspenseful.

"Why Did God Choose Jacob Over Esau?"
Genesis 25:19–34

Textual Form: Birth story.

Textual DVD: God answered their prayers and worked his purposes in ways that seemed somewhat arbitrary.

Textual DNA: A sense of personal justice or entitlement that presumes one to be favored by God because of their own merit.

Textual Focus: God exercised his choice, not by human merit but in ways that transcended human understanding.

Textual Function: To remind Israel of the sovereign purposes of God in his election of Israel.

Textual Feel: Puzzling.

Sermon Form: Narrative.

Sermon Focus: We are chosen to be a blessing to others.

Sermon Function: To remind the congregation that we have been chosen by God not through our own merit but for the purpose of blessing others.

Sermon Feel: Puzzling leading to understanding.

"Take This Job and Love It"
Isaiah 6:1–13

Textual Form: Call story.

Textual DVD: God is holy, majestic, forgiving, and pursuing his rebellious people.

Textual DNA: The need to have a calling that results in significant success and accomplishment—to make one's mark in the world.

Textual Focus: Isaiah was called to a prophetic ministry which would not be successful by worldly standards.

Textual Function: To establish Isaiah's prophetic ministry as one ordained by God.

Textual Feel: Awe-inspiring, majestic.

Sermon Form: Narrative.

Sermon Focus: Our calling is about the Caller.

Sermon Function: To motivate the congregation to look for what God is calling us to do rather than trying to determine our calling by what we want to accomplish.

Sermon Feel: Inspiring.

"The Jesus Cruise"
Mark 4:35–41

Textual Form: Miracle story.

Textual DVD: Jesus had physical need for sleep. He had power over the natural elements.

Textual DNA: The human need to cry out in panic when surrounded by immediate danger and the fear when being in the presence of the divine/supernatural.

Textual Focus: The disciples were afraid when they saw Jesus' power over the wind and the sea.

Textual Function: To identify Jesus as the Messiah who has power over the natural elements.

Textual Feel: Suspenseful, engaging.

Sermon Form: Narrative.

Sermon Focus: Jesus is in control.

Sermon Function: To encourage the congregation to trust in the power of Jesus in the midst of crises.

Sermon Feel: Suspenseful, engaging.

Appendix

"An Heir-Raising Adventure"
Luke 7:11–17

Textual Form: Miracle story.

Textual DVD: Jesus had power over death and risked being declared unclean to bring about the miraculous resuscitation.

Textual DNA: The fear that death seems to be ultimately powerful.

Textual Focus: Luke showed the powerful compassion of Jesus in the raising of the widow's son.

Textual Function: To identify the miraculous power of Jesus the Messiah over the reality of death.

Textual Feel: From sorrow to fear and wonder.

Sermon Form: Narrative.

Sermon Focus: Compassion is *real* power.

Sermon Function: To help the congregation experience the compassion of Jesus.

Sermon Feel: From sadness to worship.

"Lost and Found"
Luke 15:1–32

Textual Form: Parables.

Textual DVD: God is the one who seeks for the lost.

Textual DNA: All humans are lost in one way or another.

Textual Focus: God desired to seek and save that which is lost.

Textual Function: To call readers to repentance in order to experience the celebration of salvation.

Textual Feel: A rhythm of grief to celebration.

Sermon Form: Abductive.

Sermon Focus: God wants everyone to be saved.

Sermon Function: To call the congregation to the joy that comes from being found.

Sermon Feel: A rhythm of grief to celebration with a final unexpected twist.

Appendix

"Party with a Purpose"
Luke 19:1–10

Textual Form: Conversion story.

Textual DVD: Jesus was willing to eat in the home of a despised sinner. He came to seek those who were lost in sin.

Textual DNA: The human need to be forgiven.

Textual Focus: Luke showed that Jesus came to seek and save the lost.

Textual Function: To demonstrate Jesus' messianic mission as seeking and saving the lost.

Textual Feel: From surprise to a sense of understanding.

Sermon Form: Narrative.

Sermon Focus: We see Jesus because we are seen by Jesus.

Sermon Function: To move the congregation to gratitude for their salvation.

Sermon Feel: From surprise to a sense of understanding.

"It Is Unfinished"
Mark 16:1–8

Textual Form: Empty tomb story.

Textual DVD: Jesus had been raised. He cared for his disciples and wanted to meet them in Galilee. Jesus was able to speak accurately about the future.

Textual DNA: The fear that is normal when one encounters Jesus' resurrection.

Textual Focus: Mark ended his Gospel with the ladies being paralyzed by fear when the angel told them of Jesus' resurrection.

Textual Function: To leave the readers with a desire to finish the story in some way since it ended so abruptly with no apparent resolution.

Textual Feel: Surprising, puzzling.

Sermon Form: Narrative.

Sermon Focus: The message of Easter is meant to take us by surprise.

Sermon Function: To call the congregation to a sense of wonder and amazement about Jesus' resurrection.

Sermon Feel: Surprising, puzzling, celebratory.

"Emmaus Always Happens"
Luke 24:13–35

Textual Form: Appearance story.

Textual DVD: Christ had been raised, explained his mission from the Scriptures, and was recognized in the breaking of bread.

Textual DNA: The need for a Savior. The despondency that comes from broken dreams.

Textual Focus: Luke showed the risen Christ bringing an entirely new perspective on his messianic mission to the two disciples on the way to Emmaus.

Textual Function: To inform readers of the necessity of the death and resurrection of Jesus.

Textual Feel: From grief to surprise and celebration.

Sermon Form: Narrative.

Sermon Focus: The risen Christ gives new life to us.

Sermon Function: To call the congregation to celebrate the new life brought through the resurrection of Jesus.

Sermon Feel: From ironic to celebratory.

"Prison Break"
Acts 16:16–40

Textual Form: Rescue story/miracle story.

Textual DVD: God could bring about miraculous deliverance. His salvation brought great joy.

Textual DNA: The need to be delivered from what keeps one "imprisoned."

Textual Focus: Luke demonstrated the liberating power of the gospel.

Textual Function: To demonstrate the liberating power of the gospel so that the readers would respond to the gospel message.

Textual Feel: From despair to celebration.

Appendix

Sermon Form: Narrative.

Sermon Focus: We are saved because we are free and it shows.

Sermon Function: To bring the congregation to the point of claiming gospel freedom over what is keeping them "imprisoned."

Sermon Feel: From despair to celebration.

Bibliography

Bailey, James L., and Lyle D. Vander Broek. *Literary Forms in the New Testament*. Louisville: Westminster John Knox, 1992.
Barth, Karl. *Epistle to the Philippians*. Louisville: Westminster John Knox, 2002.
Craddock, Fred B. *Preaching*. Burlington: Welch, 1985.
Graves, Mike. *The Sermon as Symphony*. Valley Forge: Judson, 1997.
Long, Thomas G. *Preaching and the Literary Forms of the Bible*. Philadelphia: Fortress, 1989.
Lowry, Eugene L. *How to Preach a Parable*. Nashville: Abingdon, 1989.
Motyer, J. Alec. *The Prophecy of Isaiah: An Introduction & Commentary*. Downers Grove: InterVarsity, 1993.
O'Brien, Peter T. *The Epistle to the Philippians*. Grand Rapids: Eerdmans, 1991.
Platt, David, and Tony Merida. *Exalting Jesus in Galatians*. Nashville: Holman, 2014.
Wright, N. T. *Acts for Everyone*. London: SPCK, 2008.

www.ingramcontent.com/pod-product-compliance
Lightning Source LLC
Chambersburg PA
CBHW062041220426
43662CB00010B/1600